The shot seen 'round the world: The Rat Pack's publicity photo for Ocean's 11.

MOUSE

IN THE RAT PAC

The Joey Bishop Story

MICHAEL SETH STARR

Taylor Trade Publishing

First Taylor Trade Publishing edition 2002

This Taylor Trade Publishing hardcover edition of *Mouse in the Rat Pack* is an original publication. It is published by arrangement with the authors.

Published by Taylor Trade Publishing,
An Imprint of Rowman & Littlefield Publishing Group, Inc.
200 Park Avenue South, Suite 1109
New York, NY 10003

Manufactured in the United States of America

Library of Congress Cataloging-in-Publication Data

Starr, Michael, 1961-
    Mouse in the rat pack : the Joey Bishop story / Michael Seth Starr.
      p. cm.
    Includes index.
    ISBN 0-87833-277-4 (alk. paper)
    1. Bishop, Joey. 2. Entertainers—United States—Biography. I. Title.
PN2287.B4547 S73 2002
791'.092—dc21   2002006109

CONTENTS

There are many people who helped make this book a reality. I would like to thank Camille Cline and Mike Emmerich, who signed me on to write *Mouse in the Rat Pack* for Taylor Publishing and made sure the book was in good hands once Taylor was sold to Cooper Square Press. I would also like to thank my agent, Tony Seidl, who negotiated the deal and ensured this book's smooth transition from one publisher to the other. Thanks also to Michael Dorr at Cooper Square Press for his enthusiasm in bringing Joey Bishop's life story to print.

I would also like to thank those who shared their recollections of Joey Bishop with me: Marlene Ellyn, Henry Silva, Dale McRaven, Warren Cowan, Norman Brokaw, Warren Berlinger, Mel Bishop, Rummy Bishop, Dick Cavett, Sonny King, Johnny Mann, Jack Riley, Mark London, Fred Freeman, Hal Gurnee, Bill Persky, Sam Denoff, Mike Dann, Trustin Howard, Norm Crosby, Liz Kali, and Roy Baxter. Thanks also to several others who I interviewed and who might not see their quotes used in this book. You might not think so, but you were all very helpful.

I would also like to acknowledge the many journalists who covered Joey's career for years and whose work was a valuable resource, among them Bob Williams of *The New York Post*, Harriet Van Horne, Jack Gould, Richard Gehman, and reporters from *TV Guide* and *The Philadelphia Inquirer* (to name only a very few). Larry Wilde's book, *Great Comedians Talk About Comedy*, was also a valuable resource.

Special thanks also go to the photo archivists who helped me locate valuable shots of Joey: Kathy War of the UNLV Special Collections Department, Ann Limongello of ABC and David Lombard of CBS, all of whom were extremely helpful and patient. I would also like to thank Rummy Bishop, Marlene Ellyn, and Sandy Brokaw for sharing their photos. Francisco Lopez, who fought in Vietnam, graciously allowed me to use his personal snapshots of Joey visiting Dong Tam at the tail end of 1968.

Barry Dougherty of The Friar's Club in New York City helped by spreading the word, and Paul Ward of TV Land provided some valuable phone numbers (and shared "the experience" of visiting Joey in Newport Beach). Stanley Moger of SFM Entertainment provided me with numerous episodes of *The Joey Bishop Show* and many accompanying photographs, some of which I have used in this book. Thanks also to my colleague, Adam Buckman, for lending me his valuable copy of Joe Besser's autobiography, *Not Just a Stooge*. And a big thank-you to Mark Simone for providing me with a tape of his interviews with Joey and tapes of Joey emceeing Pat Brown's 1966 gubernatorial fundraiser and a 1961 Rat Pack performance at The Sands with Frank, Dean, and Joey.

I would also like to thank my mother, Zelda, who had the good sense to go into labor with me while watching *The Jack Paar Show* (don't know if Joey was on that night), and my father, Ivan, who always appreciated how hard I worked on this project. My in-laws, Toby and Sid, also helped with their support and good wishes.

Most importantly, I would like to thank my wife, Gail, and my daughter, Rachel, for their patience, understanding, and support. I slept late and was often cranky after having worked on this book until the wee hours, but they always were there to buck me up when I needed some encouragement. I love both of you very much.

The Kid from Philly

The story, as so many show-biz stories are, is probably part apocryphal, but it goes something like this: Joey was opening for Frank at the Copa, and the crowd that night, buzzing with anticipation for the Great Sinatra, was in a generous mood. Joey finished his act and was walking off the stage when he brushed past Frank.

"How were they?" Frank asked.

"Great for me," Joey shot back, "but I don't know how they'll be for you."

The timing. Joey always had the timing. Every great comedian does.

Even in birth, Joey's timing was impeccable. When he arrived in this world on February 3, 1918, the fifth child (and third son) of Jewish immigrants Jacob and Anna Gottlieb, Joseph Abraham Gottlieb set a record at Fordham Hospital in the Bronx—at two pounds, fourteen ounces (according to family lore) he was the smallest baby ever born there. (Joey's pal, Buddy Hackett: "Did you live?") Anna was fond of saying that Joey was so small she could carry him around in a cigar box.

By the time Joey was born, Jacob and Anna had been married for nine years. Anna Siegel was a stern woman, born in Romania, who was partially blind in one eye—the result of being attacked by a Jew-hating street cleaner in the old country when she was seven. Jacob, a mechanic by trade, took odd jobs where he could find them and played the ocarina to relax. Anna stayed home and raised the

1

children; oldest child Clara was followed in the Gottlieb pecking order by Morris, Harry, and Becky—with newborn Joey rounding out the household.

"Grandpa Jake was tough and was not a warm person," said Joey's niece, Marlene Gottlieb Ellyn. "But Grandma Anna was even colder. I'm probably one of the few people who did not like their grandmother. She was just not somebody who was very warm."

Jacob could fix anything with his hands, and when Joey was three months old, Jacob, looking for steady work, moved the family to South Philadelphia, where he had some connections. He got a job at the Fidelity Machine Company in Northeast Philadelphia, earning about $20 a week, and opened a bicycle shop (repairs and rentals) at 332 Snyder Avenue, moving the Gottlieb brood into a two-room apartment above the shop after a pit stop on Jackson Avenue. Joey and his four siblings shared one room, Jacob and Anna the other.

Jacob's bikes rented for 50 cents a day. Anna, when she wasn't busy with the children, often helped out in the shop.

"My mother would ask the people who rented bikes, 'What's your name?' and scribble in the book," Joey recalled. "Who knew she couldn't write English?"

The Gottlieb bike shop at Fourth and Snyder was at the heart of a close-knit, extremely territorial three-to-four-block radius that

Joey's father, Jake Gottlieb, ran a bicycle shop in South Philadelphia for over forty years. (Courtesy Marlene Ellyn)

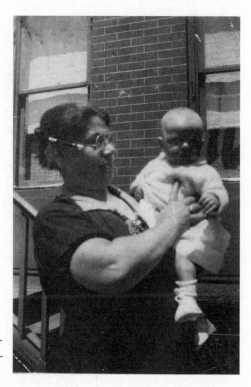

Joey's mother, Anna, holding grand-daughter Marlene (Morris' daughter). (Courtesy Marlene Ellyn)

would shape Joey's ear for comedy with its streetwise mix of Jewish, Italian, and Irish sensibilities. It was a neighborhood that would spawn the likes of Jack Klugman, Eddie Fisher, Mario Lanza, and (later) '50s teen idols Fabian and Bobby Rydell.

And it was a typically tough, self-contained inner-city enclave that protected its own—and shunned outsiders.

Joey recalled one neighborhood game called "Lay, Sleepy, Lay," in which one team of neighborhood kids hunted another team. "Sometimes, the nuts who played it, instead of just walking one block away, would wander four blocks hollering, 'Lay, Sleepy, Lay' right into an alien neighborhood—and would have to fight their way back."

The Gottliebs fit into the fabric of the neighborhood as a working-class family struggling to make ends meet ("My father sold bicycles, and who needed bicycles?" Joey said). They also followed in the time-honored Jewish tradition of joking about their near-poverty-level circumstances—laughter as the best medicine against heartbreak.

"We were poor, but how can I explain it? We were happy," Joey said. "Most comedians come from poor families, it's a struggle for recognition. We couldn't be accepted from an economic standpoint, so we tried from a humorous standpoint.

"It's like the old court jester who, if he didn't have a funnybone, would never have been in the palace in the first place."

Joey, as the youngest Gottlieb, received a lot of attention from Jacob and Anna. Jacob taught Joey the rudiments of the banjo and mandolin and versed his youngest son in Yiddish folk songs. Joey remembered buying a fake nose as a kid—the first prop for a comic who would later make his name through his verbal acuity and deadpan demeanor.

"Joey was a dreamer," Anna said. "He was always clowning, but at the same time he was very serious. Starting at the age of eight he used to stand in front of the mirror and do imitations."

Joey's first whiff of show business came when he was five. Jacob, still juggling the bike shop with his machinist's job, took the family to the Fidelity holiday show. Joey, so the story goes, sat in the first row of the balcony, watching a comedic horse act on stage break up the audience— and nearly fell out of his seat with excitement.

He was bitten. By the time he entered Sharswood Elementary School, Joey was not only watching himself in the mirror but was developing a repertoire of impersonations spanning the stars of the day: Edward G. Robinson, Ted Lewis, Fred Allen, Ben Bernie, Jimmy Durante. He would later add a monocled George Arliss, delivering a speech from *The House of Rothschild,* and also learned to tap-dance— spending countless hours on stoops with pals Henry Diamond, Ramie Needleman, and Sy Sax perfecting a soft-shoe.

"Of course, everybody in South Philadelphia could tap-dance cause when it was cold outside, it would keep us warm," Joey said. "Our group at 4th and Snyder were considered excellent dancers when it came to the jitterbug. I remember when we used to travel over to Strawberry Mansion or West Philadelphia, the girls would say, 'Oh, the South Philadelphia guys are coming.'"

If Joey was close to any particular family member in those days it was his brother Harry, who was a couple of years older and bore a close physical resemblance to his kid brother (Joey was shorter).

They shared the same aquiline nose, wavy black hair, dark good looks, and wiry frame. Older brother Morris, on the other hand, was stockier, with lighter hair and a lighter complexion. And Harry, like Joey, harbored show-biz aspirations, something in which the other Gottlieb siblings showed little or no interest. Years later, Joey would hire Harry as a "dialogue coach" on *The Joey Bishop Show*—trying to make his brother feel he was part of "the business" that would, for the most part, elude his grasp.

As kids, though, they could always dream of The Big Time, which had to be better than living above a bike shop and scraping to make ends meet. Joey had entered the Philadelphia public school system in 1924 and had proven to be quite a good student at Sharswood Elementary School. He showed a particular knack for spelling, once incurring Jacob's wrath by arriving home with 50 cents he had won in a spelling bee—and getting hit with a leather belt by his old man, who thought Joey had stolen the money. In Jacob's Central European purview, there *were* no contests—and certainly no money earned without someone using his hands.

It was the immigrant work ethic that was of its time, and Joey, like his neighborhood pals, was expected to contribute to the family coffers. That meant finding a job, or series of jobs, and Joey ran the gamut from selling peaches and tomatoes in back alleys to jerking sodas at the local drugstore to "running" phone messages to the neighbors.

"In those days . . . people here didn't have many phones. You'd call the closest drugstore," he said. "The drugstore would dispatch a runner like me to get the party. I'd make a nickel a run. Some people didn't pay up, so we didn't run for them again."

The jobs came fast and furious: making pastrami sandwiches at a restaurant at 5th and Dickinson (while mimicking the bad tippers); selling magazines and camphor door-to-door; handing out playbills; carrying ice; working in Gimbel's; dipping candles at the Pine Wax Works; and working in a luncheonette. He did anything to earn a few cents. It was The Depression. Anything and everything was needed.

Still, he found time to be a kid. In the hot summer months, Joey and his buddies would walk down to Pier 98 and swim in the Delaware River. Joey was also an excellent athlete who participated in the neighborhood baseball and basketball games. But much of

Joey's spare time was spent working on his impersonations and the rudimentary beginnings of an act. The whiff of show-biz was always in the air. He would hang around the stage doors of The Earle, The Grand, and The Colonial, trying to catch a glimpse of a vaudeville star like Benny Davis; one time, he walked more than thirty blocks, from 4th and Snyder to 5th and Lehigh, to enter an amateur contest with his lineup of impressions.

"I won second prize and $3," he recalled. "I never thought about becoming a star. I just thought how nice it was to be able to make that kind of money to help out the family."

Between the odd jobs and the time spent working up an "act," Joey tolerated school. His grades weren't exemplary, but they weren't terrible, and he managed to be elected head of the student council and vice-president of his class at Furness Junior High. Joey would always joke that he "flunked sandpile in kindergarten," but he was, in fact, a bright student, quick on his feet and always with a clever retort—qualities that would later distinguish his comedy and define his show-biz persona.

He also struck up a lifelong friendship with Sister Joan Marie, a nun who taught at Our Lady of Mount Carmel School in the neighborhood. "I was playing handball and looked over at Mount Carmel and thought, boy, they had a much better wall to play against," he said.

"So I went over to play and Sister came out, and I was going to go but she told me I could stay. I said, `But Sister, I don't go to this school. I'm Jewish.' And she said that was OK, I could play there." When Sister Joan Marie, who was then ninety-three, became ill in 1996 and knew she was dying, she instructed those around her to immediately alert Joey.

By the time he entered South Philadelphia High School, the show-biz bug that had bitten Joey Gottlieb years before had blossomed into an all-consuming obsession. It was great to joke around with the guys in the neighborhood, shooting pool at 7th and Morris, but Joey, always thinking a step ahead, knew he needed a bigger stage if he was ever to realize his ambitions. He had already won the "Benny Goodman Jitterbug Contest" in 1936 (free passes to Atlantic City's Steel Pier for a year!) and wanted more. Remaining in high school was not an option.

So he dropped out.

How this decision affected Jacob and Anna remains unclear; in later years, Joey mostly glossed over his decision to abandon high school, preferring to discuss his entrée into the burlesque circuit. But the fact that he was eighteen when he dropped out, and technically an adult, likely gave Joey the leverage he needed (at least with his parents) to begin his show-business career in earnest. Still, Jacob and Anna couldn't have been thrilled that their son didn't have a steady job.

After dropping out of high school, Joey journeyed north to New York. He was going to take the town by storm while bunking with relatives on the Lower East Side. But the best he could do was a two-week gig as an emcee at a Chinese restaurant on Broadway. He wore a tuxedo, which he rented from a distant cousin in the business, and rode the subway to work, keeping his stage makeup on so people would know he was in "the business." Each day he packed two sandwiches, since the owners of the Chinese restaurant refused to feed the help. For all that, and little more, Joey earned the princely sum of $13 a week.

He had the ambition.

Now all he needed was an act.

"Mad Maniacs of Mirth and Mimicry"

They called him "Rummy," but his real name was Morris Spector. He lived a couple of blocks away from Joey, but the two boys didn't really know each other well; although separated by less than a mile, the territorial world of South Philadelphia was marked by landmarks and unspoken agreements. Go two blocks and you were OK; go a few more blocks and you entered an entirely different neighborhood (at your own risk). "If you lived within one block you knew everybody," said Rummy, "but a guy could live two blocks away and you never heard of him."

Rummy Spector earned his nickname from his nose, "a fairly good proboscis" as he called it. He remembers getting hit by a snowball when he was a kid, his nose "lighting up like a red balloon" and some wiseacre named Simon Aaronson, who lived down the street, nicknaming him "Rum Nose." The nickname stuck and, over the years, evolved into just "Rummy."

Rummy, like Joey, harbored show-business aspirations and had worked up an act with pals Ramie Needleman and Sammy Reisman. They called themselves "The Three Rs" and when they weren't entertaining at parties, they hung out at the Neighborhood House on 6th and Mifflin, where they goofed off, worked on "the act," and entered various local talent contests, with spotty results.

"Everybody had a club, where they met with a sponsor, and I belonged to a group called the Brower AC, which met at the Neighborhood House and had a basketball team and a baseball team," Rummy said. "They also had drama there, where we put on plays once a year and had contests for the best play."

Frank Tonkin, who ran the drama club at the Neighborhood House, had a suggestion for "The Three Rs," who were looking to expand the act.

"He said he'd heard of a guy over on Snyder Avenue named Joseph Gottlieb—he was called Joseph in those days—who did impressions and would be great for us," said Rummy. "So Frank Tonkin was the one who brought us all around and introduced us to Joey."

In the hundreds of newspaper and magazine articles written about Joey after he became famous, that fateful meeting of Gottlieb, Reisman, Spector, and Needleman is a one- or two-line mention. It shouldn't be. That meeting would be the most important meeting of Joey's career.

Ramie Needleman soon dropped out of the act, leaving Joey, Sammy, and Rummy to make it on their own. Gottlieb, Reisman, and Spector didn't exactly smack of glitzy show-biz, so the boys thought long and hard about what to call themselves. Their savior came in the way of Glenn Bishop, one of the few black kids in the neighborhood. Glenn had been friends with Rummy for years.

The story repeated time and again by Joey was that Glenn Bishop let Gottlieb, Reisman, and Spector borrow his car, with the proviso that they would use his surname for their act.

"Joey says that but it's not true," said Rummy. "Glenn had less money than we had and was just a struggling guy, so he didn't have a car. He just hung around.

"Glenn was my best friend in grammar school, and when he saw us put the act together he said to me, 'Why don't you take my name? It will take you straight to the top!' We were looking for a name, so we became the Bishop Brothers."

The Bishop Brothers now had an official name. All they needed was some work—and an act.

"Our first gig, I believe, was at a place called O'Shea's Wagon Wheel, a one-nighter in Philly, and we got our pictures in the paper for that," said Rummy.

But it was Frank Palumbo who gave the Bishop Brothers their first big break. Palumbo ran a place over on Catherine Street called Palumbo's, well known in Philadelphia for featuring star performers, including Jimmy Durante. Palumbo hired the Bishop Brothers for about $45, or $15 apiece—pretty good money in those days.

For their act, Joey, Sammy, and Rummy borrowed heavily from the era's pop culture, particularly from *The March of Time*, a newsreel series that had begun three years earlier. Shown in theaters before the big feature, *The March of Time* featured stentorian narrator Westbrook van Voorhis delivering news of worldwide events. It would eventually be parodied by Orson Welles in the *March of Time* newsreel footage shown in *Citizen Kane*.

"We would act out the news but we made up our own news," recalled Rummy, who now called himself Rummy Bishop. "But what we really had was excitement. Our opening was that we would always be late; we would have the emcee announce us, the band would play our theme—and nothing would happen. Then, about the third time they played the music we would start our fight coming in from the door with our suitcases and overcoats, arguing. 'This ain't the place! I told you it's your fault we're late!' What we did, we had no real act so we had to make excitement.

"Before we got into *The March of Time* we'd sing 'California Here I Come,' and one guy would holler out, 'Did you hear the latest?' And we'd take out our newspapers and do news items. And we also got into a fight with the bandleader."

"We did impressions, and bad ones at that," Joey said. "Just before we were introduced, Frank Palumbo passed out newspapers. So when he came on stage everybody was reading. I said, 'Hey, what's this, the Free Library? So they drowned us. There was a chorus line on the bill, six gorgeous heads who came out with parasols and did 'Singing in the Rain' with special effects in the background—rain compliments of the plumbers union.

"Jack Curtis was the emcee and halfway through our act he told the rainmaker to turn on the car wash. Now, I wouldn't say we got wet, but the next week we got jobs as lifeguards in Atlantic City."

If the Bishop Brothers weren't exactly world-beaters, their stint at Palumbo's did give them some valuable on-stage experience. It also earned them enough notice to snag a job at Mike Dutkin's

Rathskeller on Broad and Girard—which, in turn, led to their first longstanding gig.

"Joey was always the spokesman for the group, he did all the business," said Rummy. "The owner at the place on Broad and Girard said he would give us $45, so Joey says to him 'We'll take it on one condition: We get top publicity here.'"

Rummy, Freddie Bishop (center), and Joey (right) with some seated nightclub pals (1938). (Courtesy Rummy Bishop)

"Well, Hitler had just invaded Czechoslovakia and the owner got mad and said, 'I'll tell you what I'm gonna do, I'm gonna take Hitler right off the front page and put you guys there. All three of you, get the hell outta here!'"

On their way out of the joint, the boys were stopped by Maxim, the male half of French dance team Maxim and Odette, who were playing the club at the time.

"Maxim said he was taking a show to Buffalo and was looking for comedians. So he drove us to Buffalo in his car," Rummy said. "I'll never forget that on the highway he got a blowout and the car was swerving as he drove off the highway. I remember his wife said to him, 'You *vanna* roll?'"

And that's how the Bishop Brothers ended up at the Havana Casino in Buffalo, where they opened on September 12, 1938. It was their first important gig.

"Havana Casino presents The Show of Shows!" read an ad in the local paper. "Gorgeous Girls in a Colorful Revue! Internationally Famous Vodvil [*sic*] Acts! What a Cast! What a Show! See the French Parade, the March of Time and the Gypsy Camp; the Bishop Bros.; 3 Mad Maniacs of Mirth and Mimicry—they're crazy—they're nuts— they're a riot; Maxim and Odette, internationally famous French dance team; direct from New York City and European nightclubs."

The bill was filled out by Darlene De Chante ("lovely singer of songs"), Helen Sinclair ("dancing on skates") and The 4 Pomponettes ("gorgeous, enticing girls, thrilling, different").

It didn't take long for the Bishop Brothers to be spotted by Harry Altman, who owned a club in Williamsville on the outskirts of Buffalo. Altman upped the boys' pay to $75 a week and kept the Bishop Brothers for about a month. They played Williamsville long enough to get a nice, small write-up in *Variety*.

The *Variety* review caught the eye of a talent agent in Chicago, who sent the boys a wire inquiring if they were interested in coming to the Windy City for work. Joey, Sammy, and Rummy showed the wire to a local talent agent, Wally Gluck, who promised to handle the Chicago deal.

"He was asking about $100 a show and set us up with an agent in Chicago," Rummy Bishop remembers. "But when we got there, the agent wanted us to audition. So Joey says, 'You mean you brought us all the way here to do an audition?!' But he said they had buyers who would come and select the acts they wanted, so we did the audition."

The Bishop Brothers, with Buffalo and Williamsville already under their belts, were good enough to attract some interest and were chosen to open at a hotel in Chicago, where they got their $100—and promptly got the boot after a few nights.

"That was the only job we got and now we were starving in Chicago," Rummy recalled. "We all couldn't leave the [hotel] room at the same time because they'd close the door and we couldn't get back in, so one guy had to stay in the room at all times."

Joey, Sammy, and Rummy, out of work and with no prospects, were forced to write to their parents back in Philadelphia, asking them to send money for the boys to return home. But instead of returning to South Philly, Joey, Rummy, and Sammy decided to give Buffalo another crack, and took a bus there instead of going home. Once in Buffalo, their luck once again took a turn, and they were offered a chance to work in Detroit, at a place called The Bowery.

The headliner at The Bowery was Harvey Stone, a comic who had won some acclaim for an Army routine, which he had also performed on radio. But Stone had gotten a local girl pregnant, and—trying to save his career—was offering "a tremendous amount of money," according to Rummy, to one of the Bishop Brothers if he would agree to marry the girl. Joey and Rummy passed on the offer—but Sammy was considering it. He remained in Detroit to think it over while Joey and Rummy went back to Philadelphia without any prospects on the horizon.

Once back home, however, Joey got restless to hit the road again. Sammy was still in Detroit, but Joey was convinced the act could go on without him. In the late spring of 1939 he called Mel Farber, a guy from the old neighborhood, and asked him to join the act, replacing Sammy. Although he was three years younger than Joey and Rummy, Mel had been on the fringes of show business since he was 13, working as a singing waiter in Atlantic City. Mel agreed to join the act—and became Mel Bishop.

The reconfigured Bishop Brothers didn't have to wait long to get another offer. With Mel now on board as the act's straight man, they

The Bishop Brothers cut loose at the South Mountain Manor in the summer of 1939. Left to right: Mel, Joey, and Rummy. (Courtesy Rummy Bishop)

headed for the South Mountain Manor House to be the summer-staff entertainers, leading hikes for guests when not doing their show. The Manor House, a summer lodge located outside of Reading in Wernersville, Pa., was owned by Eddie Gottlieb, the South Philadelphia basketball whiz who helped form the NBA. For the Bishop Brothers, the summer of 1939 would prove to be a slam-dunk.

"I remember they offered us $30 a week, so Joey says, 'We'll take the $30 if you throw in the laundry,'" Rummy recalled. "We stayed there the whole season as the house act. During the week we ran events."

"We stayed there through Labor Day and for that we made the magnificent sum of $50 apiece," says Mel Bishop. In their spare time, the boys would goof around by lip-synching to Andrews

Sisters records, and considered incorporating the lip-synching routine into the act. They never did. "Me, like the schmuck that I was, said we have talent, we don't have to do other people's records," recalled Mel Bishop. "So we didn't do it." A decade later, a young comic from Newark, New Jersey, named Jerry Lewis would attract some attention—by lip-synching to records.

The club at the South Mountain Manor was big enough to draw the attention of agents from Philadelphia, who would drive out on Saturday nights to scout local talent. One agent liked what he saw in the Bishop Brothers and offered them the real deal: Twelve weeks on the so-called "Eastern Wheel" of the burlesque circuit, which would take them by train to cities such as Union City, Newark, Boston, Detroit, Dayton, Cleveland, St. Louis, and Pittsburgh.

"It was a tremendous experience," Mel Bishop recalled. "The big comic on our first show was Maxie Furman and his straight man was Herbie Barris. They used us in their skits, which was fantastic, because from these guys we learned timing."

The boys were required to do three shows a day, one at noon and 2:30 P.M. then another show at 8:30 P.M. The act, more or less, was the same as before, with the boys singing "California Here I Come" and then launching into the *March of Time* shtick. Joey and Rummy did their impressions while Mel played the guitar and acted as straight man.

"[The act] consisted of satires on radio programs," Joey said. "*Lights Out, We the People, Gangbusters.* Rummy did all the commentator impressions—Boake Carter, Westbrook Van Voorhis, the *March of Time* voice. Mel sang and I did all the comedy and dramatic impressions. In those times, there were local agents, like Pete Iodice in Detroit, Al Nortin in Rochester. They used to put you in with a revue. Like, they had the Bishop Brothers and the Eight Cocktail Girls. We would augment the revue."

It was customary, in those days, for the chorus girls on the burlesque circuit to "choose" who they wanted for male companionship during the twelve-week run. There was a lot of down time, with tedious train rides and lots of time to kill between shows in faraway cities most of the performers had never dreamed of visiting. For some, it was their first time away from home. For most, it was a chance to indulge in the opposite sex.

Mel Bishop recalled one such adventure in Pittsburgh.

"We were staying in Pittsburgh in a room with three beds—Joey in the middle and Rummy and me on the other sides," he said. "Joey had been trying for weeks to do something with this one girl. We all went up to the room and talked, and finally Rummy and I went to bed. And Joey and this young lady really went to it, and when it was over, Rummy and I turned around and applauded.

"Joey, being theatrical, got up and took a bow, then put his hand down. He wanted the girl to take a bow—but she didn't want to."

Down in Baltimore, the boys worked a place called The Subway, managed by a gravelly voiced character named Slim Pavese. Joey endeared himself to the tough-talking Pavese each night by sneaking up behind one of the women singers, getting under her dress and popping a flashbulb—emerging with his face soaking wet. "The boss loved it," Mel said of Pavese.

The Bishop Brothers followed Pully and Hump on the Subway bill. Pully and Hump, a popular vaudeville act at the time, was fronted by B. S. Pully, who would later go on to co-star in the movie version of *Guys and Dolls*. But all the goodwill and hard work Joey, Rummy, and Mel put in at the Subway and elsewhere was thrown into chaos when Mel decided to leave the act soon after the Bishop Brothers returned from the twelve-week Eastern Wheel burlesque tour.

"I felt funny . . . I fit into the act, but I wasn't doing comedy and I was a little bit uncomfortable," Mel said. "We came to the conclusion that if I left the act they would see what happened without me."

Despite the Bishop Brothers being cut down to a twosome, Joey and Rummy were delighted to be offered a spot on yet another twelve-week Eastern Wheel tour, to which they agreed. Joey's brother Harry would drive the boys to some of their jobs in his white convertible. Harry now called himself Freddie Bishop, since he was an honorary Bishop Brother (and thought Freddie sounded better than Harry). In return, Joey would often get his brother a job waiting tables at whatever club the boys were entertaining. Several years earlier, Freddie had opened up a pool hall down the street from Jake's bike shop, but his partner was busted for running numbers and thrown in jail. So Freddie was available for work. He would spend the better part of the next two decades working as a maitre d'.

"When Freddie drove us to a club, Joey always made sure he got put on as a waiter there," says Rummy. Joey would later dub his brother "Freddie the Hook," for the way in which he hooked his hand out behind his back for a tip.

Freddie drove Joey and Rummy to Al Mercur's Nut Club in Pittsburgh, where the two Bishop Brothers received rave reviews in the local papers.

"Al Mercur has a satire and impersonation act winner in those Bishop boys, Joe and Murray, in his Nut House," the *Pittsburgh Sun-Telegraph* enthused on March 27, 1940. "Murray," in this

Joey, "Boogie Woogie" Sherman, and Maxie Simon at Boogie Woogie's Nut Club in Pittsburgh (1938). (Courtesy Rummy Bishop)

case, was Rummy, who sometimes switched his name around for the hell of it.

The Pittsburgh Press, in its "Bright Spots" column, ran an item on wacky "Kernel" Mercur's club—illustrated with a photo of a smiling "Joe" Bishop.

"As if one screwball at a time isn't sufficient for anybody, Al Mercur has started booking them in pairs for the nightly high jinks at his Nut House . . . This time it's the Bishop Brothers who bring more zany stuff to the 'insanitarium.' Last year the Bishops were a trio, and played one night at Mercur's spot . . . However, as they had some time to idle away Mercur enabled them to get a paying job for the layoff."

A week later, Joey and Rummy—along with actors John Garfield and Harry Carey, then starring in *Heavenly Express*—were featured in a show staged by the American Legion Post of the Variety Club at the Veterans' Hospital.

"Garfield was an immense hit in one of the scenes from *Heavenly Express,* and Carey was a great favorite in a monologue both humorous and instructive," read a review in the *Sun-Telegraph.*

"Al Mercur's Nut House contributed the very funny impersonators, the Bishop Brothers, who work on the order of Chick and Lee."

Al Mercur, meanwhile, had been telling Joey and Rummy about his brother Lou's joint down in Miami Beach, which was also called the Nut Club. Al put in a call to his brother to tell him about the Bishop Brothers and, with Freddie behind the wheel of the white convertible, Joey and Rummy set off for Miami, hoping to find work for the winter season.

"We were a big hit in Florida because Joey had a knack of saying the right thing at the right time," said Rummy. "We were at a club in Miami Beach called the Wit's End, where every Monday night they had all the acts in town come in and do ad-libs and shtick.

"Well, one of the big things going on at that time was a fight against the musician's union; the musicians wouldn't play certain songs because they weren't getting royalties. So Joey gets up on the stage, turns to the band and says, 'May I have a restricted G chord, please?' The place fell apart. He always said something the people would talk about."

Sometimes, he said too much. One night, working Lou Mercur's Nut Club, Joey and Rummy closed out the evening by dancing with a couple of girls. Joey tried sweet-talking one of the girls into inviting him up to her room, even though she had a baby ("We'll be very quiet," Joey assured her). Nothing happened.

Several days later, Joey and Rummy were on stage at the Nut Club when suddenly Rummy noticed something from the front table, where two couples were seated.

"This guy sitting ringside lifts up the tablecloth and he's flashing a gun," Rummy said. "I motioned to Joey so we started acting nuts—the audience didn't know why, but they were laughing.

"When the show was over the guy sends for me and says, 'Remember those girls? Who was with who?'"

The "guy" was Ralph "Boots" Capone, a minor Chicago mobster who lived in his kid brother Al's shadow. Rummy convinced "Boots" that nothing had happened with the girls—one of whom happened to be Capone's wife.

"So he says, 'Can Joey take a joke?' So he grabs Joey by the collar, shoves him against the wall and pulls out a gun and says, 'Were you with my wife?' The place starts emptying out and Joey's brother, Freddie, comes out. So Freddie walks over to break it up and Ralph, like a little baby, puts the gun away and says, 'Okay.'"

Joey and Rummy played the Nut Club for most of 1940, dragging out the old *March of Time* routine night after night, peppering the act with impersonations and riffs on news of the day. In the audience one September night was Sylvia Ruzga, a pretty blonde from Oak Park, Ill., who was working the winter season in a nearby Miami Beach hotel. ("Since Sylvia is not Jewish, I still can't figure out what she was doing down there at that time of year," Joey joked.) Joey often told of how, between shows, he spotted Sylvia in the audience and went over to introduce himself. "You must be a comedian," she said to him, "but I haven't seen you do anything funny." It was love at first sight.

Joey and Sylvia were married on January 14, 1941, and four months later Rummy received a letter from Uncle Sam and entered the Army under the peacetime draft in May 1941. He would never again work with Joey as part of an act. The Bishop Brothers were history.

Joey was now down to a solo, an unfamiliar situation and one that caused him some anxiety. "I was nervous at first," he said. "Rummy had always supplied the punch lines, but as soon as I walked out there I knew it was going to be all right. I felt free, relaxed."

Despite losing his comedy partner, Joey slogged on, finishing the gig in Miami Beach and, in July 1941, wending his way north with Sylvia to Cleveland—and to a place called El Dumpo. Really.

If El Dumpo was known for anything but its name, it was for its bartender, Joe Gorcey—the father of *Bowery Boys* actor Leo Gorcey.

"He saved me from getting killed there one night," Joey recalled. "Out in the audience was a guy named Game Boy Miller, who—unbeknownst to me—was one of the top-ten most wanted men in America.

"Here he is with five other guys and some broads, and just as I was preparing to step on stage, the owner of the club came up and whispered to me, 'Game Boy Miller is here celebrating his birthday. Wish him a happy birthday. So I said, 'Okay.'

"I walk up on stage and say, 'Ladies and gentlemen, we have the celebration of a birthday tonight.' And I start singing 'Happy Birthday' . . . no sooner did I get out the words 'Game Boy' than a bottle flew past me. The guys he was with grabbed me and were taking me into the washroom when Joe the bartender stepped in and said, 'Listen, the kid did not know.'"

But working El Dumpo proved to be a valuable training ground. "In the clubs, it's a matter of attack or be attacked," Joey said. "Also, since I weighed 135 pounds in the early days, I was in no position to attack."

Without a partner to work off of, Joey had to rely on his quick wit and sharp ad-libs. His dour, world-weary demeanor only added to the effect of throwing off a sharp line with the shrug of a shoulder—"to be *overheard*, rather than heard," he'd say, "almost as though you think you are the only one who heard what I have said."

Whatever it was, it worked. Joey played El Dumpo at $100 a week from July 1941 through April 1942, when he was drafted into the Army and assigned to Special Services at Fort Sam Houston in San Antonio, Texas.

Joey would spend the next three-and-a-half years there, earning a promotion to sergeant and being made Director of Recreation. While at Sam Houston he also took up boxing, a lifelong passion that began when he was a kid, ushering fights in Philly.

At Fort Sam Houston during that time was the great Fritzie Zivic, "The Croat Comet," who defeated Henry Robinson for the welterweight crown in 1940, beating Robinson again in 1941. Zivic began training Joey, who was always in excellent athletic shape and had the lean, wiry build of a welterweight contender.

Zivic thought Joey had the stuff to become something of a fighter and started Joey on a serious training regimen. Under Zivic's tutelage, Joey became a skilled boxer—skilled more at evading matches than actually winning one, although he eventually won the welterweight boxing championship of the Eighth Service Command. "I won it by default," he said. "It's the only way to do it—especially if you're yellow."

Joey was only half-kidding. In his first match, arranged by Zivic much to Joey's horror, his opponent failed to show up, and Joey was declared the winner. This happened again in Joey's second bout— no opponent, Joey winning by default—and, amazingly enough, a third time, when both Joey's opponent and the alternate failed to materialize.

Finally, in the welterweight finals, Joey actually fought a flesh-and-blood human being—a guy who had just returned from a three-day furlough and was nearing exhaustion. He was the perfect opponent for Joey the novice boxer.

"I was boxing a guy who had professional experience," Joey said. "Zivic kept telling me that the guy lowered his right hand from time to time. 'When he lowers his hand, close your eyes and swing hard.' I didn't close my eyes, but I swung—and you know what? I knocked the guy out. It was almost like a movie.

"I still don't know where he got the names of my opponents," Joey said. "They weren't in the Army records."

After leaving the service and returning to the club circuit, Joey was approached in New York by a fight manager who wanted him to quit show business and turn pro. "I'll turn fighter when you can find a matchmaker like Fritzie Zivic," Joey replied.

Joey relived his boxing experiences years later on *The Joey Bishop Show*, when he laced up with heavyweight Jerry Quarry, who was about to fight Muhammad Ali. As the men jokingly "swung" at each other, Joey inadvertently hit Quarry—not hard, but enough to enrage Quarry, who snarled on live TV, "Nobody hits me in the fucking face, not even in fun!"

The steadiness and predictability of Army life agreed with Joey, especially after the previous four years grinding it out in clubs up and down the East Coast without a steady paycheck.

"It was the most security I had ever felt," he said later about his Army experience. "I wanted to be a permanent Army man. I kept thinking, what am I looking for in life? And I kept answering security, a good income for my wife, a school for my kids. The Army offered all this. Show business was such a struggle."

Sylvia's health was also a major concern. Sylvia had undergone three serious operations while Joey was stationed in San Antonio, all of them performed in civilian hospitals. Now, news of a much-needed fourth operation forced Joey into making a decision that would alter his career.

Worried about how he was going to pay Sylvia's hospital bills on his Army pay, Joey applied for an emergency discharge in August 1945. His request was granted, and Joey was discharged from Brook General Hospital, Fort Sam Houston. He and Sylvia decided to remain in San Antonio for the time being. Joey would go back to the nightclubs working as a single—reviving the act that had carried him through the year in Cleveland at El Dumpo.

He found a few gigs in and around San Antonio, most notably at a place called the Mountain Top Diner, run by Captain and Mrs. Talmadge.

"I stayed there twelve weeks, until my wife was well," Joey said. "In the meantime, Bob Lee, an orchestra leader who was working the St. Anthony Hotel in San Antone [*sic*], went up to the Mountain Top Club and he called the [William] Morris office about me, said, 'I saw a kid that would be very good.' So they sent me a wire and said, 'When you leave San Antone [*sic*], let us know.'" At this point, El Dumpo wasn't looking so bad.

Joey's luck turned when an agent from William Morris called, offering Joey a gig at a two-bit club called The Casablanca Roadhouse, just outside of Philly. It was a start. Joey and Sylvia trekked back to South Philly, taking an apartment over Kaplan's Butcher Shop across the street from Anna and Jacob, still running the bike shop.

Joey was welcomed back into the old neighborhood, setting its sights for the first time on his blonde, exotic, *goyishe* wife from Illinois—that distant land of wheat and WASPs.

"You have to understand that South Philadelphia was very provincial," said Joey's niece Marlene, the eldest daughter of Joey's brother, Morris. It was Marlene who, after they returned to Philly, became somewhat of a surrogate child for Joey and Sylvia.

"Sylvia was very glamorous," Marlene remembered. "Here was this show-businessy lady . . . who was so different than South Philly. She was glamorous to us, and she decorated their place as much as you could decorate the second floor of a butcher shop. I was in awe of her. I used to do her roots.

"Joey and Sylvia didn't have any children and I was kind of like their child," Marlene said. "They would take me to all of these places where Joey was performing. There were movie houses in those days that would have a feature film and a stage show in-between screenings. Joey and Sylvia even took me to my first circus."

Being back home was nice, but Joey was working clubs that still weren't up to snuff. The Casablanca Roadhouse, for starters, was certainly no picnic. Joey remembered one night when gun-toting crooks broke into the place, one of them breaking a woman's jaw with the butt of his gun while ordering Joey to keep talking ("I did the same Edward G. Robinson impression 35 times," he said).

But he plugged along, until he got a call in 1946 from a William Morris agent. It was the break he was looking for: a week at The Greenwich Village Inn in Manhattan for $125. Joey jumped at the offer. The last time he worked New York was the miserable Chinese-restaurant experience nine years before. Then, he had limped back to the bike shop hat in hand.

This time, things would be different.

Joey headlines The Strand Theatre in New York (1950).

3
CHAPTER

"The Frown Prince of Comedy"

The Greenwich Village Inn on Sheridan Square was a landmark club. Founded in the 1920s, it was considered by most performers to be a springboard to bigger and better things (Tony Bennett was discovered there in 1949 by Pearl Bailey). For Joey, his booking there represented a huge break. It wasn't so much the money—which was more than he had made since going solo—but the fact that this was New York City, the epicenter of show-biz. Performing at The Greenwich Village Inn meant being seen by the "right" people, smart, sophisticated types who could help launch a performer's career simply through word-of-mouth. It wasn't the Copacabana, but it was a far cry from El Dumpo and "Kernel" Al Mercur's Nut Club.

But now, the impressions that Joey had relied upon during his time with Sammy, Mel, and Rummy weren't much of a factor in his act. And certainly the *March of Time* routine had to be dropped. (Mort Sahl, newspaper in hand, would create his own, unique take on the *March of Time* shtick in the late 1950s.)

Joey's act had evolved—more through necessity than any forethought—from physical comedy to more thoughtful observations couched in his unique style of sarcasm and pointed observations. Working as a solo meant he had to rely on his wits alone; there was no one else who could bail him out. "I call it an open mind," he explained of his on-stage attitude. "I just go out and talk. I don't have any mental file of jokes. If I did I wouldn't ad-lib.

"It's usually based on adversity," he said. "My own adversities or those of others. I don't set the adversity. Usually it suggests itself."

So Joey now began to riff on his poor childhood in South Philly ("My folks were poor, but I didn't mind poverty because we always played games. For instance, when I'd come home sometimes they had moved to another address"). If he wasn't getting laughs, the audience became a target ("Last night the crowd was so quiet we held hands and tried to contact the living").

"Well, I could always do the impressions," he said. "I did Cantor, Jolson, Edward G. Robinson, James Cagney, Fred Allen. I used them as a crutch for comedy. I originated lines like, 'Cagney—five thousand a week and he can't afford a belt.' I do what I call 'thought humor.' If the thought went through my mind, I'd go out and do it without writing it."

His mantra—"to be *overheard*, rather than heard"—played well to the more sophisticated New York audience. The word-of-mouth spread, and Joey's one-week engagement at The Greenwich Village Inn turned into an eleven-week run.

"I worked there with Joan Barry, then [radio personality] Barry Gray came in for four weeks," Joey said. "He did a show as a comic. As a matter of fact, he had all the jokes written and he read them and as each one bombed, he threw it on the floor. When I followed him, I picked them up and said, 'You should read the other side,' and I pretended to read the jokes from there."

But what should have been the start of a burgeoning New York nightclub career screeched to a halt. Although Joey had proven to be somewhat of a draw, receiving a few good write-ups in the New York papers, he was out of options once The Greenwich Village Inn gig ended and no other offers were on the table.

So now what? Chicago was a possibility, although Joey's experiences there with Mel and Rummy six years earlier hadn't exactly set the world on fire. But Chicago was, after all, Sylvia's hometown, and she hadn't been home in a while. So what the hell? With little to lose, Joey's agent at William Morris booked him at the Vine Gardens, located on Chicago's North Side. Sylvia was going home.

Once again, Joey's timing proved serendipitous. His act at The Vine Gardens went over big, and they held him over for forty-nine weeks. Bandleader Russ Carlyle, meanwhile, was in town at Chicago's biggest club, Chez Paree, considered the major leagues for any nightclub performer. Three years younger than Joey, Carlyle, twenty-five, had gotten his start as a vocalist with Blue Barron before forming his own band in 1940 (which his sister, Louise, ran for three years when Russ was drafted into the Army in 1943). Carlyle, who billed his band "The Romantic Style of Russ Carlyle," liked what he saw of Joey's act and invited Joey up on stage to do some shtick with the band. It stuck. Joey was booked at Chez Paree—the first comic in Chicago nightclub history to make the leap from a "neighborhood" spot like The Vine Gardens directly to the big time. Joey ended up working at Chez Paree for forty-nine weeks with singer Tony Martin, pulling in $1,000 a week—huge money for *any* club comic in those days. When he had the time, Joey worked gigs in other Chicago clubs like The Oriental.

"Even Danny Thomas, as successful as he was, had to leave the 5100 Club and go to the Martinique [in New York] and then come back to the Chez. It was a policy they had," Joey said.

"I became curious as to how I would open, 'cause I had just come from a neighborhood spot and now I'm going to the Chez Paree, so curiosity started my wheels going. Then I dealt with honesty. And the routine I came up with was:

Ladies and gentleman, I am here through the generosity of you people. For forty-nine weeks I worked at the Vine Gardens and every night one of you nice people would come and say, 'What are you doing here, why aren't you at the Chez Paree?' I feel after tonight's appearance, a lot of you are going to say, 'What are you doing here, why aren't you at the Vine Gardens?'

It was in Chicago that a wag at the Chez Paree bestowed upon Joey a nickname he hated—dubbing the dour-faced comedian "The Frown Prince of Comedy" for his world-weary demeanor. (Jack Paar would later describe Joey's visage as that of "an untipped waiter.")

And now there was a baby on the way. Because of Sylvia's health problems, she and Joey never expected to have children. But while they were in Chicago Sylvia had become pregnant. "It was a big surprise to the family," remembered Joey's niece, Marlene. "They had been married for quite some time, and it was a big surprise when she got pregnant." Son Larry was born in Philadelphia on August 4, 1947. Joey, the boxing fan, remembered Larry being born "the night Ike Williams fought."

With another mouth to feed, the pressure to find work increased. Now back in South Philly, and with successful runs in New York and Chicago under his belt, Joey found it easier to get booked into surrounding clubs like Chubby's (where he was described as "the young man with the troubled manner"), The Celebrity Room and The Latin Casino in Cherry Hill, N.J.

"Sad-faced, sad-voiced Joey Bishop, a comic who deserves the biggest breaks, is the new Latin Casino star," read a November 1950 review. "Bishop has a smart, sophisticated routine with fast lines and sharp, timely gags; and he offers novel and uproarious impressions, the victims being Ted Lewis, Peter Lorre, and an old-fashioned soft-shoe dancer. Supporting Bishop is the new recording star, Tony Bennett, who sings a variety of tunes with lilt and verve."

"Joey Bishop . . . is back at the Latin Casino after a year in Chicago, a town which has more or less adopted him," reported *The Philadelphia Inquirer*. "The solemn-faced comedian has moved right on into the big time and he had to beg off from the beguiled dinner audience last night.

"Nothing succeeds like success and Joey's run at the Chez Paree put the finishing touches on this act. We always thought Joey was amusing and now he's good. He even wears a tuxedo, as becomes his new stature in the nightlife world. He works exceptionally clean and his impersonations, which deliberately misfire, are welcome for a change."

With Joey and Sylvia back home, the extended Gottlieb family pitched in to help with the baby. Niece Marlene, about ten years older than her baby cousin, became Larry's official babysitter.

"I babysat Larry every day after school—that was my job," Marlene recalled. "He was an absolutely gorgeous child, and Sylvia had me come after school from 3 to 6 P.M. and I would baby-sit for him."

The work kept on coming, the club dates running into months and then years as Joey seesawed between gigs in New York, Philadelphia, and Chicago. Roy Baxter—an acquaintance from the old neighborhood whose real name was Roy Gottlieb—wrote some material for Joey. Baxter then submitted the jokes to Joey's manager, Chubby Goldfarb. "I don't know if he ever used it, but I did see

Joey when he was appearing at The Strand Theatre, where he was the entertainer for the week opening for a John Wayne movie," Baxter said. "I remember distinctly Joey was so strong that he got a standing ovation. He went offstage and came back holding a baby, which was his son, Larry. They went over to the microphone and Joey turned to Larry and said, 'Larry, the church is on fire.' And Larry says, 'Holy smoke!'" I have never forgotten that."

Backstage at The Strand with actress Denise Darcel, putting in a good word for Hebrew National (1951).

4

CHAPTER

"Sinatra's Comic"

It was now 1952 and Joey was wondering if he would ever be more than a pretender to the throne. He was earning a decent living working the clubs, but there had to be more. He was beginning to develop a love-hate relationship with the lifestyle—loving the money he earned (he was now up to $1,000 a week) but hating the travel and loneliness that came with the territory. "There isn't a lonelier life in the world," he said later. "I was always a stranger in town."

Out in Hollywood, Frank Sinatra was in the midst of his spectacular comeback, filming *From Here to Eternity*. The onetime Bobby Soxer idol had seen his career nearly destroyed, first by losing his voice and then by leaving his wife for Hollywood sexpot Ava Gardner. Sinatra's tempestuous relationship with Gardner had alienated his fans, and a string of forgettable movies hadn't helped Sinatra's cause. But his role as the doomed Maggio in *From Here to Eternity* would earn Sinatra an Oscar and single-handedly resuscitate his career. Just a year before he had been performing for half-empty crowds in Vegas and begging for TV work; now, he was selling out the Paramount. It was 1942 all over again. Sinatra was unstoppable.

Joey had always admired Sinatra from afar. Who didn't? Although they had never worked together on the same bill, Joey and Frank had played some of the same clubs through the years, sometimes missing each other by a matter of days or weeks. By 1952, Joey had spent nearly fifteen years on the club circuit, getting a whiff of the big time but never quite putting it all together for the Big Payoff. The Greenwich Village Inn and Chez Paree had tantalized and

The young comic strikes a pose while performing as the stage act for Clash by Night *at the Paramount in New York (1952).*

teased, putting Joey on the cusp of big-time stardom only to yank him back down when the engagements ended and the next big thing failed to materialize.

Television, meanwhile, was making huge strides in helping introduce comics to millions of people. Ed Wynn, Milton Berle, Bob Hope, Martin & Lewis, and Red Skelton had all adapted their acts to television. Joey, however, wasn't big enough to warrant any television exposure or even the occasional radio appearance.

Still, despite the seemingly overwhelming climb, Joey pushed on, always managing to pull himself up, dust himself off, and throw himself back out there, ready and willing to work anywhere, any-time. It was the life of a club comic. Still, the disappointments began to take their toll. Joey's blunt attitude, honed through the years, now took on a smattering of cynicism. He wasn't taking anything for granted. Ever. And that also applied to Sinatra.

"Once, when I was sharing a bill with Frank at the Copacabana, the audience kept me going 28 minutes overtime almost every night," Joey said. "Frank kept telling me, 'You're solid now, you're on your way.' Know what happened? I didn't work for six weeks!"

But his resilience paid off. In 1952, Joey was booked into The Latin Quarter, the fabled Manhattan nightclub on 48th and Broadway run by Lou Walters (father of Barbara Walters). Sinatra, in town at the time, caught Joey's act and liked what he saw. Sinatra appreciated Joey's no-bullshit attitude, the way he seemed to shrug off the audience, almost as if he didn't care what they thought of his patter. Sinatra was only two years older than Joey and sensed in the comic the same fierce independence he himself possessed. It was that hard shell, developed through years of per-forming on the club circuit. And Sinatra had heard the Joey Bishop stories making the rounds. The best-known tale concerned the time in 1946 when Joey followed Danny Thomas at a New York policemen's benefit in Madison Square Garden. Thomas, a master monologist, left the crowd in stitches, and Joey had the unenviable task of following another comedian—never a good thing. So what did Joey do? He walked out onto the stage, coat over his shoulder, and leaned into the microphone. "What Danny Thomas said, that goes for me, too," he proclaimed, and sauntered off the stage. The crowd loved it.

Joey and Sinatra had met, but they hadn't yet worked together. That changed when Sinatra asked Joey to open for him at Bill Miller's Riviera, a plush club in Fort Lee, New Jersey, that attracted the smart New York City set—some who might have remembered Joey from his Greenwich Village Inn stint back in 1946.

"I didn't know the [Riviera] stage revolved, and on opening night, Frank pushed me onto the stage," Joey recalled. "And when the stage didn't stop, Frank said to the crowd, 'Place your bets, 'cause I don't think he's gonna stop!'"

"Frank spoke of my talents when you could get a good argument," Joey said later. "He saw me working in some third-rate joint and he took me into his act at the Riviera in 1952. It was the first time I was in a 'class' club and the first time the right people saw me work.

"Frank knows I'm not a fast act. I need time," he said. "On different occasions, Frank has talked a club manager into giving him less time on the bill and letting me have 25 minutes instead of 18."

Sinatra urged Joey not to change his act and was impressed enough with the "Frown Prince" that he made sure Joey opened for him whenever he was in New York—and sometimes even on the road at places like Skinny D'Amato's 500 Club in Atlantic City.

As Sinatra's star continued to rise, it had a residual effect on Joey. In the incestuous world of show business, Joey was perceived to have Frank's blessing; he was "Sinatra's comic," which was tantamount to writing his own ticket to the top. Doors that were once unapproachable now opened more readily; Joey was booked into the hot Manhattan nightspots including The Copacabana, where he opened for Sinatra and drew big crowds even when Sinatra wasn't on the bill.

And Frank took care of Joey in other ways.

"Frank made a Western, his first Western and not a very good picture, called *Johnny Concho*," recalled Warren Cowan, Sinatra's longtime publicist, who also handled Dean Martin, Sammy Davis Jr., and Peter Lawford.

"I remember calling Frank in Spain, where he was doing another film, and I said why don't we take *Johnny Concho* back to the Paramount and have a special premiere? Because that's where Sinatra became Sinatra.

"Well, Frank called me back a couple of days later and said I've topped you—I'm gonna play the Paramount for a week. And he was able to get Tommy and Jimmy Dorsey to join him; they hadn't talked to each other for years. And he said he'd found this young comic named Joey Bishop to open the show for him.

"I was there for the opening, and Joey became an immediate sensation and got a lot of attention and generated a lot of excitement and a lot of press," Cowan said. "I remember being in a car with Sinatra and asking him why he didn't manage Joey. 'You found him, you discovered him, shouldn't you own him or have a piece of his future?' And he said, 'No, I don't want to get into that. But Joey's on his way and he's going to make it.' Which indeed he did."

Joey always pointed to one particular appearance with Sinatra, at The Copacabana in 1954, as a sign he had "made it," at least in the tough world of nightclubs.

"Frank asked me to open for him at the Copacabana. He had just won the Oscar for *From Here to Eternity* and was hot again," Joey said. "The place was mobbed. I came out, sized up the place, and said, 'Look at this crowd. Wait till *his* following shows up.' In the middle of my act, Marilyn Monroe walks in all by herself, draped in a white ermine coat, and of course, all heads turned toward her.

"I looked at her and said, 'I told you to sit in the truck.' That stopped the show. At ringside, sitting together, were Victor Jory and Gabby Hayes. I introduced them and said, 'For a minute, I thought I was watching the late, late show.'

"Following the first performance, I went over to Lindy's and when I walked in the whole place went crazy. After that, I was on my way."

But it wasn't to be an overnight success story. Joey continued to play the clubs—New York, Chicago, Miami, and elsewhere. He joined a USO bill that entertained troops during the weekend at Travis Air Force Base in northern California, working alongside Debbie Reynolds, Howard Keel, Keenan Wynn, and Arthur Loewe Jr.

Although he was making a name for himself, Joey never believed anything would last. He took whatever jobs he could—no matter what the venue.

"When my husband and I got married, my husband was stationed in Fort Ord," remembered Joey's niece, Marlene. "Joey was appearing at a nightclub there called Bimbo's that featured a naked girl who swam around in a fish tank."

The New York Post lauded Joey in a May 1954 review, the article highlighted by a caricature of Joey's hangdog face.

"Lillian Roth is back at La Vie Rose, heading a show that features comedian Joey Bishop, a new foursome called the Footnotes, and the June Taylor dancers," Martin Burden wrote. "Bishop, a skinny guy with a gentle, low-pressure comedy style, is an ingratiating entertainer. 'If you're not lucky as you go through life,' he advises, 'CHEAT.' He sniffs the cigaret *(sic)* smoke wafting through the room and announces solemnly, 'Somebody here is under arrest.'

"Joey considers himself an unlucky comedian. 'Who else,' he asks, 'gets booked into Boston during Holy Week . . . into Las Vegas during the Atom Bomb tests . . . into Miami during August?'

"'My agent, he adds, 'doesn't want to waste me. He's saving me for something big—color radio.'"

The good press, and Sinatra's stamp of approval, was hard to ignore, and now Las Vegas began taking notice. Joey began his life-long association with Sin City during this period, working the Desert Inn and the Copa Room at the Sands—future home of the Rat Pack.

The bigger venues naturally meant more money. Joey was now pulling in a six-figure salary, and in the mid-fifties he and Sylvia bought their first house, a seven-room white-brick colonial in Englewood, N.J., a stone's throw from Manhattan.

They enrolled Larry in public school and formed a coterie of Englewood friends including comics Buddy Hackett, Phil Foster, and Dick Shawn. John Griggs, who would later co-star on *The Joey Bishop Show*, was a neighbor. Joey had always enjoyed golf, and he now began playing in earnest, purchasing a percentage of the Englewood Country Club along with Hackett, Foster, and Shawn. The trio per-formed frequently at the club, helping to boost its profile by bring-ing in celebrity friends (Ed Sullivan, Perry Como, Phil Silvers, Sammy Davis Jr., Tony Bennett) to shoot a few rounds. Larry excelled in school and played Little League (third base), while Sylvia settled into the suburban routine, beginning a collection of Fabergé eggs.

The club dates were coming fast and furious now. Joey was working regularly at The Copa, where a 1959 review of his show with newcomer Andy Williams labeled Joey "a debonair master of funny lines . . . Bishop has a nonchalance that is a disarming cush-ion for his comic thrusts. When you least expect it, he'll throw out a telling line that has the customers fanning the air with delayed-action laughter when they had been looking for a change of pace."

The proximity to Manhattan also meant less traveling and more work in a medium that had thus far eluded Joey: television. His association with Sinatra had transformed Joey into one of the country's "hottest" club comics, but that success had failed to cross over into television. It was a fact that irked Joey to no end, especially after eight appearances on *The Ed Sullivan Show* in 1956 failed to attract other TV offers.

"Today, the club comics are competing against the greatest, who are seen regularly on television," he griped to the hometown *Philadelphia Inquirer* in a 1956 interview ("TV No Laughing Matter to Club Comics Today," read the headline).

"They are seen for free, too, and then guys like me have to come in to a club and do it for money. The people have to pay to see us. It isn't that people's tastes have changed. They haven't. But look at it this way: When I worked the Latin Casino or the Sands in Las Vegas . . . I had to compete with the guy who worked the spot the week before.

"But today, with television, they see the Berles, the Gobels, and the Gleasons all week. And I'm competing against them. Those guys are free. We have to come in and do it for money!"

But all that was about to change.

In the spring of 1958, Joey was approached to do a guest spot on the new CBS game show *Keep Talking*, hosted by Monty Hall (later of *Let's Make a Deal* fame). *Keep Talking* would be shot at CBS in New York. Always thinking ahead, always analyzing, Joey figured he would be seen by more people in one night of television than he would through years of club dates. He decided to take a gamble, foregoing nine months of club work—and nearly $200,000 he would have earned—to appear on *Keep Talking* for only $850 per week.

It turned out to be the shrewdest gamble of his career.

"I've turned down $4,000 a week from unimportant clubs for *Keep Talking*," he said at that time. "Money is not the important thing to me, thank God. I'm thinking about a career now and I think being exposed on TV is the most important thing."

Keep Talking divided its weekly collection of six celebrities into two teams. One player on each team was given a secret word and had to tell an improvised story using that word—with the other team trying to guess which word it was. The show relied, naturally,

With Danny Dayton on the CBS version of Keep Talking, *1958.*

on verbal acuity—Joey's forte. He shined on *Keep Talking* from Day One, overjoyed (even for the "Frown Prince") to be departing from the hoary riffs and impersonations of his nightclub routine to a fresh, anything-goes approach each week. And he was finally introduced into America's living rooms—legitimized, if you will, by his stellar *Keep Talking* colleagues Orson Bean, Morey Amsterdam, Paul Winchell, Danny Dayton, Ilka Chase, Pat Carroll, Peggy Cass, Elaine May, and Audrey Meadows.

Joey's appearances on the ABC game show Keep Talking *in 1958 helped make him a household name. That's host Merv Griffin (left) with panelists Danny Dayton, Peggy Cass, and Paul Winchell (top row) and Joey, Pat Carroll, and Morey Amsterdam (bottom row). (Courtesy ABC Photography Archives)*

More importantly, Joey felt that *Keep Talking* underscored his "everyman" appeal as the dour *schlub*. And it gave him the opportunity to perpetuate two of his cardinal show-biz rules: Have an *identity* and have *attitude*. If he came across on *Keep Talking* as a mournful wise ass—"*overheard* rather than heard"—so be it. By Joey's estimation, a comic pushing for laughs "destroys the very attitude he's worked so hard to create. He's not a genuine comic then.

A genuine comic is a guy who's told by the audience that he's funny. The other kind is the guy who tells the audience that he's funny.

"My cynicism is based upon myself," he said. "I don't tell audiences to be cynical. I just bring them down to reality. On *Keep Talking*, they wanted me to smile at the signoff. I refused. I wouldn't stand in their way if they'd wanted to change the format, but don't change me."

Joey figured his "what me, worry?" shtick was an attitude with which most of America could identify. He was the bike-shop-owner's son from South Philly who somehow found himself on national TV, wearing a tux and playing a silly game.

"Viewers are getting a lot sharper, and demanding more subtle material," he said. "What they accepted some years ago is old hat now. Look what happened to a lot of comics that were on TV a while back—gone, that's what. And why? They were never developed into personalities, human beings. The performer who wants to get anywhere in TV has to be down-to-earth and real to viewers, like Jack Benny . . . overpowering nightclub comedy won't stand up on TV because you run out of material too fast. On television you can't keep topping yourself."

He was right, of course. And even if he was wrong, who was going to tell him? Nearly twenty years of working the club circuit had hardened the "Frown Prince," who added to the hardscrabble image by cropping his once-wavy hair into a buzzcut ("It just looked funnier," he said by way of explanation).

Joey had always been opinionated, but he took on an almost defensive posture now that he was finally being recognized after working his ass off in every two-bit joint from Miami to Pittsburgh. Journalists who interviewed Joey once he hit it big on *Keep Talking* often couched their feelings about him in descriptive terms ("abrupt," "direct," "challenging"). But at least he was honest and practiced what he preached. If you didn't agree with Joey, then fuck you. He knew what was best for his career. And no one was going to tell him otherwise.

"How do people feel about me? I'm not concerned about that," he said. "It's how I feel about them. To thine own self be true, right? To be accepted because of this, and not in spite of it . . . this is what I want."

Joey's exposure on *Keep Talking* generated reams of news clippings on this "overnight" discovery, but the show itself was by no means a ratings success. Its low viewership numbers were compounded by a change of hosts—Carl Reiner replaced Monty Hall shortly after the show's debut—but that didn't seem to make any difference. *Keep Talking* was nominated for an Emmy, which saved it from extinction, but then it moved with its third host, Merv Griffin, from powerhouse CBS to weakling ABC—still in its infancy and without the affiliate muscle of CBS or NBC.

But if Joey's club work had caught the eye of his first big benefactor, Frank Sinatra, his weekly appearances on *Keep Talking* caught the attention of the next man who would further his career: Jack Paar.

5

CHAPTER

Enter Jack Paar

Jack Paar had succeeded Steve Allen on NBC's *Tonight Show* in July 1957. Unlike Allen, Paar wasn't a comic, didn't do sketches, and didn't surround himself with an ensemble of wacky comics. Paar's gift was the gift of gab, and he was more comfortable conducting thoughtful interviews than creating characters.

Paar had gotten his start on radio in the 1940s as a summer substitute for Jack Benny, and worked his way through a variety of TV and radio gigs until NBC came calling.

Paar was a master monologist—moody, introspective, mercurial—who was as likely to tell stories about his daughter Randy or share tales of his latest trip to Africa as he was to interview intellectual giants like Albert Schweitzer or Jonas Salk. He could be demeaning, supportive, dismissive, cutting, and extremely funny—Joey's mirror image. America was fascinated by the Paar enigma and made *The Jack Paar Show* (as it was now called) appointment viewing for 90 minutes each weeknight. In its heyday, the *Paar Show* averaged about 35 million viewers a night. Appearing with Paar was the video equivalent of a mention in Walter Winchell's column. It could make or break a career.

While Paar didn't rely on a supporting comedic ensemble, he did have his favorites—actors, comedians, and raconteurs who constituted his "regulars" during his five-year run on NBC, among them Elsa Maxwell, Cliff Arquette (a.k.a. Charlie Weaver), Peggy Cass, Alexander King, Hans Conried, and Buddy Hackett.

In 1958, Paar added Joey to the list. He had seen Joey on *Keep Talking* and appreciated Joey's no-nonsense approach to comedy and his lightning-quick ability to ad-lib. If Sinatra had lifted Joey into the better clubs with the "right" people, it was Paar who would turn Joey Bishop into a household name (at $320 a pop) and would later write about Joey in his 1961 memoirs, "My Saber Is Bent."

When Joey first came on our show he had been knocking around in clubs for years without getting anything on fire, including the crepes suzette. In no time at all, it seemed, he was star, making pictures, joining Frank Sinatra's clan, getting his own TV series and acting as emcee for the $100-a-head inaugural gala for President Kennedy.

'I'm now working in places,' he told me, 'where a year ago I couldn't afford to go' . . . Joey has a wonderful knack for self-editing. One night he sat for a half-hour on our panel without saying a thing. Finally he raised his hand. 'Yes, Joey?' I inquired. 'Nothing, Jack,' he said. 'Just wanted you to know I was still here.'

Asked time and again to name the biggest influences in his career, Joey always named the same three men: Frank Sinatra, Danny Thomas, and Jack Paar.

"For something like 21 years I've been trying to make people laugh," Joey told an interviewer in 1959. "I've appeared in clubs everywhere . . . and it was only last summer after I appeared on the Paar show that people gave me a second look. I'll tell you why—on that show I was real to them. I was myself. I wasn't pushing hard for laughs.

"And it has paid off for me," he said. "For in two recent club appearances—one in Chicago and one in Philadelphia—I broke attendance records for the rooms in which I performed. I was also pleased by the type of audiences I drew. A number of parties were made up of families who knew me strictly from seeing me on TV. I met people who had driven in from Racine, Wis., who, a year ago, had never heard of me. These are people who ordinarily don't go to nightclubs but, thanks to TV, came to know me and were nice enough to come to see me in person."

Paar loved him, writing in his memoirs that,

Despite his success in nightclubs, Joey was not well known nationally until the exposure on our show introduced his wry talents to a mass audience. He was an immediate hit. Joey is one of the quickest men on the comeback I know. One night we talked about Pavlov's experiments with dogs in Russia. I explained that by ringing bells when they fed the dogs, and then ringing bells and not feeding them, the Russians caused the animals so much anxiety they went insane.

'Maybe they weren't trying to drive the dogs nuts,' Joey suggested. 'Maybe they were just trying to train the bell.'

Hal Gurnee was Paar's producer. "Joey wasn't well-known when he first came to the show. Standups in those days didn't have the clout they have today," Gurnee said. "I was taken by how quick Joey was, everybody noticed that. He was like a hawk; he would sit there, and whatever Jack said, whatever anyone else said, he had a comeback.

"He never initiated anything," Gurnee said. "It was always the counterpunch with Joey. I never saw anybody do that before—it was like the wiseguy in the back of the classroom who had something to say but nothing to contribute."

Joey's semi-regular appearances on the Paar show, coupled with his continuing weekly appearances on *Keep Talking*, opened up other TV doors. He was now welcomed on the top-rated *Perry Como Show* (four times) and *The Garry Moore Show*, guested on shows hosted by Sinatra, Esther Williams, Polly Bergen, and Dinah Shore and even did a dramatic turn on CBS's *Richard Diamond, Private Detective* playing—what else?—a club comic (opposite Mary Tyler Moore's legs).

"TV has been wonderful for and to Joey," columnist Jack O'Brian wrote in the *New York Journal-American*. "He works masterfully on *The Jack Paar Show*, where he can exercise the greased-lightning mentality which twinkles to whatever topic or random event is served up, however casually. Behind that shrewd false front of no-expression races a comic mind attuned to the topical call of impudent small talk. He is a comic counter-puncher, at his best in quick-phrased rejoinder, at his worst sermonizing or psychologizing."

The TV work was enough to generate a small amount of interest in Hollywood. Claudette Colbert had caught Joey's act in Vegas and recommended him for the part of Ali Hakum in the movie version of *Oklahoma!* It didn't work out. But movie producers liked what they saw in Joey, who wouldn't be able to carry a picture but could certainly add a touch of "attitude" to a smaller role. In quick succession, Joey was cast in small, forgettable roles in three World War II–themed movies in 1958: *The Naked and the Dead,* an adaptation of Norman Mailer's 1948 novel; *Onionhead,* a followup to *No Time for Sergeants* starring Andy Griffith; and *The Deep Six,* starring Alan Ladd as a Quaker pacifist who grapples with his beliefs when called into active duty.

Joey never considered himself an actor and said as much ("There are too many guys around who have studied their craft so well that they make me look like a novice"). But the roles, however minor, played off his newfound TV fame and broadened his exposure. It couldn't hurt.

"Felicia Farr does well as the love-hungry, frustrated Stella, and Erin O'Brien is neatly decorative as the object of Mr. Griffith's noble affections," *The New York Times* noted in its review of *Onionhead.*

"Joe Mantell, as an ex-barber with a penchant for saving his mates' hair; Joey Bishop, as a dame-chasing gob . . . and James Gregory, as the skipper, add a few realistic bits to the proceedings."

Of the three movies, *The Naked and the Dead* held the most promise ("I play both parts" was Joey's stock quip). The popularity of Mailer's novel, encompassing a doomed Army platoon in the South Pacific, had generated a lot of buzz as Hollywood undertook translating Mailer's book to the big screen. The movie sported an impressive pedigree: action director Raoul Walsh (replacing Charles Laughton), screenwriter Norman Taurog, and a score by Bernard Herrmann. Its stars—Cliff Robertson, Aldo Ray, Raymond Massey, and Richard Jaeckel—had compiled a large body of work among them.

Joey spent ten weeks working on the movie. Eight of those weeks were spent on location in Panama.

Gossip columnist Dorothy Kilgallen wrote that *The Naked and the Dead* would do for Joey what *Sayonara* had done for Red Buttons—re-shape the comic in a dramatic light. Buttons, though, had copped an Oscar for *Sayonara.* Joey was having none of that. "I got the part because they wanted a fellow around 34, with big ears, short-cropped hair, and a voice that could pass for Brooklyn or Strawberry Mansion," he said when the movie opened. "I fit the description."

Joey played Private Roth, the token Jew in a platoon of central-casting soldiers led by psychotic, Jew-baiting Sgt. Croft (Ray), who delights in prying gold teeth out of dead Japanese soldiers and hallucinates about killing his stripper wife. Croft is kept under the watchful eye of Lt. Hearn (Robertson) but eventually dooms the platoon. Roth meets his maker when he sprains his ankle in a hail of gunfire; dragging himself up a hill, he's taunted by a sneering Croft ("Your kind always tries something like that"), tries to leap across a chasm and plunges to his death.

"In the book, he was a no-guts guy until the climax of his Army career," Joey said of Roth. "In the movie I'm a bird lover. When we hit the beach for the first time, I see a bird and I bury it quickly. It's a terrific scene, I think.

"All through the picture I sacrifice my real feelings for humor. The character just sort of developed as the movie went along. That's the way it often happens, I understand."

"The praiseworthy effort to produce a giant of a film from Norman Mailer's towering World War II novel, *The Naked and the Dead,* has resulted in a professionally turned but derivative action drama no more memorable than similar sagas of strife that have preceded it," *The New York Times* noted. Director Raoul Walsh has filled the screen with striking vistas in beautiful color and with the chilling sound and fury of conflict, but the heart, minds, and motives of men exposed to sudden and often useless death, which gave the book its awesome power, serve merely as sketchy background to battle in this uneven picturization. . . . As portrayed by Aldo Ray in rough-hewn, laconic style, [Sgt. Croft] is the standard, hard platoon leader seen in more than one movie.

"The other members of the detail are competent, but also appear to have been chosen solely to represent the types that comprised our citizen army. There are, to name a few, Joey Bishop, as the wry, comic Jew; L. Q. Jones as the hillbilly cutup who is the darling of a strip-teaser and the platoon for whom he brews "jungle juice"; there is the hard-bitten, cynical loner played in dour fashion by Robert Gist . . ."

Although Joey was now talking about the "respect" of being a movie actor ("Once you've acted in a picture, people accept you as

Joey guest-stars with his hero, Jack Benny, on The Jack Benny Show *(November 1960). Benny would later return the favor by guest-starring on* The Joey Bishop Show. *(Courtesy CBS Photo Archive)*

an actor and you're that as well as a comic"), he realized his destiny was on the small screen.

"TV is the only medium," he said almost defensively. "There is nothing else. If you're a hit in a picture, it doesn't mean anything today. And only a few nightclubs matter. It doesn't mean anything anymore to be a hit in Pittsburgh or Des Moines. Those people can see you on TV."

Millions of people watched Joey's idol, Jack Benny, on TV every week. *The Jack Benny Show* was an institution on CBS, and Benny was one of the few vaudeville comics to embrace television and actually make a go of it. He earned a new generation of fans with his brilliant timing, patented double take, "stinginess," and bad violin playing. Joey had worshipped Benny from afar for years, and was shocked to hear that Benny—who had seen him on *Keep Talking* and on *The Jack Paar Show*—was now telling anyone who would listen that "Joey Bishop is the smartest young comic around."

"Joey Bishop is one of the funniest men I have ever seen," Benny said. "He's just naturally a funny man. Great ad-lib comedian. Thinks fast. A lot of people think he worries too much; I think so, too, but then this you can't stop. That's his style but he's great."

But Benny's admiration didn't end there. In the fall of 1958 Joey, playing The Sands in Vegas, was halfway through his act when a man in the audience stood up and complained loudly, "I'm going home. You're too funny—and too young." It was Benny, of course, who was performing down the street. Later that week, Joey found out why lines had suddenly begun forming for his late show at The Sands: Benny, at the end of his act, was telling his audiences to rush over to see Joey, "The funniest young comic in the business."

Jack Paar legitimized Benny's proclamation in May 1959, when he turned his show over to Joey for a one-week guest-hosting gig—the first time anyone had ever guest-hosted for Paar. NBC had actually approached Joey several months before to pinch-hit for Paar during his vacation, but Joey turned them down ("I didn't think I was well-enough known," he said).

"Now that I've had some exposure on Paar's show, I will do it on the basis of doing a favor for a friend who's away on vacation," he said, accepting NBC's offer the second time around. "I'm a little like Paar in a few respects, I think. One of the things that makes him interesting to viewers is his attitude of tiredness and boredom.

"So long as I can keep things informal, I think I'll be all right. I plan to play it like I do when I'm a guest on the program—the reluctant-to-be-here attitude."

Joey's guests, lined up by Paar's staff, included Larry Storch, Faye Emerson, Buddy Hackett, *Onionhead* co-star Andy Griffith, and pal Phil Foster.

"Actually I'm dreading it a bit for one reason," Joey said before the first show. "For the past 20 years I've been telling all my friends, 'If I can ever help you out, let me know.' Now, I'm in the spot where I can and, believe me, has my phone been ringing!"

Joey was kidding, but he kept true to his word, inviting old comedy partner Rummy Bishop on as one of his first guests. Joey and Rummy reminisced about the old days, which were apparently of little interest to Paar's studio audience, who fussed and fidgeted through this trip down memory lane. "It was just one of those nights," Joey said later. "We couldn't buy a laugh."

But guest-hosting *The Jack Paar Show* was simply the fuse leading to Joey's bombshell breakout in the fall of 1959, at a star-studded roast of Dean Martin at the Friar's Club in Los Angeles. The easygoing Martin, much to everyone's surprise (and joy), was going great guns after his messy breakup with Jerry Lewis. Now, the likes of Frank Sinatra, Danny Thomas, Phil Harris, Danny Kaye, George Burns, George Jessel, Bob Hope, and Eddie Cantor were ready to give him shit for it—the ultimate Friars compliment. "Everybody important was there," said Joey—who paid his own way to fly in for the occasion.

Joey was seated inconspicuously at the end of the dais, almost as an afterthought, partly hidden by a palm tree (or candelabra, depending on who's telling the story). Adding insult to injury, he was going on first—a comedian's nightmare, especially in such stellar company. And he only had four minutes to impress his colleagues.

He didn't waste any time. The lines came fast and furious.

"They put me in an end chair, where I had the choice between speaking to a Spanish-speaking waiter or to Mort Sahl, who I understood less than I understood the waiter."

"I also sat next to sweet, wonderful Dinah Shore, and she spoke to me all night. Things like 'Pass the butter,' 'Where's the salt?'"

[Turning to Danny Thomas]: "You had so much faith in your nose. You wouldn't have it operated on. So now they're filming the Durante story, and who's got the lead? Dean Martin!"

[Motioning to Steve Allen]: "I've never worked for you, nor do I intend to. I've seen what's happened to your people on TV. Don Knotts is a nervous wreck. Tom Poston can't remember his name. Skitch Henderson hasn't time to shave. If you're that kind of taskmaster, no thanks!"

Singer Sonny King had roomed with Martin for six years in the early '40s. He and Jimmy Durante, who King was touring with at the time, were at the Martin roast sitting in the front row.

"Joey gets up and says, 'I want to thank you, Mr. Sinatra, for putting me behind a palm tree; all I saw was a vision of Dorothy Lamour,'" King recalled. "He went on and on about that palm tree, and everyone was hysterical. He went from $10,000 a week to $40,000 a week after that."

King might be embellishing Joey's fee a bit, but not the reaction to Joey's performance. The next day Joey's phone rang off the hook with offers: four TV shows, guest-starring roles and movie offers. Hal Wallis, who had directed Martin and Lewis, offered a big-screen contract. Joey turned them all down. He had more important fish to fry. Sinatra had asked Joey to appear in the new movie he was putting together. It was a heist caper he wanted to film in Vegas, in and around the Sands, with a group of pals—something called *Ocean's 11*.

Keeping cool at The Sands during the filming of Ocean's 11: *Frank, Dean, Sammy, Peter, and Joey.*

6 CHAPTER

Four Kings and a Joker

The script for *Ocean's 11* had been brought to Sinatra by Peter
Lawford, a Sinatra acquaintance since 1946, when they had
worked together on MGM's *It Happened in Brooklyn*. Sinatra
and Lawford ran in the same Hollywood circles for several years, but
in 1951, the mercurial Sinatra cut Lawford off after a dinner-party
set-to involving a woman ("some hokey misunderstanding,"
Lawford said). They didn't speak again until 1958. By that time,
Lawford had married Patricia Kennedy, sister of Massachusetts senator John F. Kennedy. Sinatra, always drawn to power, was intrigued
by Lawford's Washington connections.

The plot of *Ocean's 11* revolved around a gang of eleven Army
buddies, led by ringleader Danny Ocean, who hatches a plan to rob
five casinos in Vegas (The Riviera, The Sahara, The Flamingo, The
Desert Inn, and The Sands) simultaneously. Lawford had shopped
the script around Hollywood but found no takers until meeting
Sinatra at a party and describing the plot, which Sinatra loved (he,
of course, would play Danny). They quickly made amends, opened
up a Beverly Hills restaurant together called Puccini's and went
about casting *Ocean's 11*, which they sold to Warner Brothers
Sinatra referred to his new pal as "The Brother-in-Lawford" and, to
demonstrate his loyalty, helped land Lawford a role in *Never So Few*,
a World War II drama in which Sinatra was starring with Gina
Lollobrigida.

With Sinatra on board, *Ocean's 11* was a done deal. Veteran
director Lewis Milestone (*All Quiet on the Western Front*) was hired

Spyros Acebos (Akim Tamiroff) outlines the Ocean's 11 heist plan to Danny Ocean and his crew.

to direct the picture, and soon thereafter Sinatra pals Dean Martin and Sammy Davis Jr. were enlisted as co-stars. Martin had resurrected his post–Jerry Lewis career with an impressive turn in *The Young Lions* and combined a take-no-shit attitude with a blase demeanor—forever winning Sinatra's respect. Frank never fucked with Dean.

But that wasn't the case with Sammy, who had met Sinatra in 1940 when he was touring with his father and uncle as the Will Mastin Trio. Like Lawford before him, Davis had incensed Sinatra, earning banishment from the inner circle by criticizing Sinatra's behavior—and his singing(!)—during a Chicago radio interview. "Talent is not an excuse for bad manners," Davis said. "I love Frank, but there are many things he does that there are no excuses for." Word quickly got back to Sinatra, who had had *Never So Few* rewritten to include a black character custom-tailored for Davis. Sammy could forget about the part now; Sinatra, who was said to own a copy of Sammy's infamous Chicago interview, cut him off cold— ignoring Sammy for the better part of a year, refusing to speak to or see him and giving his part in *Never So Few* to Steve McQueen. Sinatra finally relented when Davis literally begged his way back into Frank's good graces ("T'was reported that Sammy was ready to hurl himself prostrate on the stage to ask Frank's forgiveness," wrote columnist Earl Wilson). Sinatra rewarded Sammy with a role in *Ocean's 11*—as a singing garbage man. Frank had made his point.

And, so Fritzi Zivic's boxing lessons shouldn't go to waste, Joey was assigned the part of Mushy O'Connors, an ex-boxing champ and one of Danny's eleven Army buddies. Norman Fell, Jerry Lester, Richard Conte, Henry Silva, Richard Benedict, and Cesar Romero rounded out Danny Ocean's "eleven," with veteran character actor Akim Tamiroff in a supporting role.

Joey tied up his loose ends so he could focus on the movie, which was to begin filming in January 1960 in Las Vegas, with a six-week production schedule. An additional five weeks in Los Angeles was pencilled in for additional scenes.

Sinatra's brainstorm to film *Ocean's 11* in Vegas met with some resistance from local authorities, who feared the scene in which Danny and his boys plunge Sin City into total darkness by cutting the power, might give the locals some ideas. But Sinatra won them over and moved the production to The Sands, a piece of which he owned along with Martin. The Sands would serve as the movie's home base—not only for the fictional *Ocean's 11* characters but for a real-life show-business happening that would electrify Las Vegas, turn the entertainment world upside-down, and give birth to The Rat Pack.

The "Rat Pack" term had been coined in the mid-'50s by Lauren Bacall, whose husband, Humphrey Bogart, liked to drink and carouse with a gang that included Spencer Tracy, Katharine Hepburn, John Huston, Judy Garland, agent Irving "Swifty" Lazar, and Sinatra, who idolized Bogey (but had eyes for Bacall all the same). Bogart, by this time, was gravely ill battling the cancer that would eventually kill him. Still, the gang congregated almost every night in the Bogarts' Holmby Hills home to drink and talk, and before long had developed into a kind of society that dubbed itself "The Holmby Hills Rat Pack," complete with a set of rules.

"It really stood for something," Bacall later told *Life* magazine. "We had officers. Bogey was Director of Public Relations and I was the Den Mother. We had principles. You had to stay up late and get drunk, and all our members were against the PTA. We had dignity. And woe betide anyone who attacked one of our members. We got them." Garland served as first vice president; her husband, Sid Luft, was the pack's cage master, while Lazar was the recording secretary and writer Nathaniel Benchley the historian. Sinatra was the packmaster.

Now the packmaster, two years after Bogie's death, was getting restless. He missed the old Holmby Hills Rat Pack days and thought he might re-create some of the old magic while shooting *Ocean's 11* in Vegas. Sinatra declared to the press that he would convene a "summit conference of cool," which was soon shortened to "The Summit." So what was "The Summit" going to be? By Sinatra's definition, "The Summit" would be a party the likes of which no one had ever seen before—at least in Vegas. By day, Frank, Dean, Sammy, Peter, and Joey would shoot *Ocean's 11;* by night, they would hold court in the Copa Room at The Sands, performing a freewheeling show that seemed ad-libbed. In reality, the show

The Summit at The Sands, January 1960: Some of the Ocean's 11 cast (George Raft, Richard Conte, and Henry Silva, left to right) join Dean, Frank, Joey, and Sammy on stage. Peter is partially hidden behind Frank. (Courtesy Sands Hotel Collection, University of Nevada, Las Vegas Library)

Dean, Frank, and Joey awaiting their cue backstage during one of The Summit shows.
(Courtesy Sands Hotel Collection, University of Nevada, Las Vegas Library)

would be carefully scripted by Joey, who would also serve as emcee (and sing the occasional song—badly).

Sinatra's announcement of The Summit set off a frenzy for tickets to the nightly shows. It also caught the attention of the national press, which dispatched newspaper and magazine reporters to witness The Summit and explain to the rest of America what it meant to be "cool." Belmont Books took it one step further, commissioning journalist Richard Gehman to write a quickie book about the phenomenon, calling it *Sinatra and His Rat Pack: The Irreverent, Unbiased Uninhibited Book about Frank and 'The Clan.'* Gehman devoted a chapter of the book to Joey.

In just a matter of days, the Copa Room became the epicenter of universal cool. Joey emceed the nightly shows before a packed house of gamblers and celebrities, including, one night, Peter's brother-in-law, Senator John F. Kennedy. Kennedy told Joey he had been a Joey Bishop fan for years. On other nights, stars such as Harry James and Joe E. Lewis were called up on stage to partake in the shenanigans and the "in" show-biz jokery.

In February, *Time* magazine devoted an entire page to The Summit shows, headlining its article, "Joey at the Summit."

On every table in the big nightclub at Las Vegas' Sands Hotel, a card announcing the night's entertainment carried as an after-thought: "Oh yes . . . and Joey Bishop." Joey's thin, sad face glooms out of the card's corner as if he felt the same way. Theoretically, Joey has bottom billing—fifth man after the show's four stars. But happily, as soon as he starts talking, he is recognized as top banana in a newly assembled comedy act that is breaking up Vegas. His fellow performers: Frank Sinatra, Dean Martin, Sammy Davis Jr., and Peter Lawford.

"Who's starring tonight?" asks the M.C. as he opens the five-cornered show. Joey's voice is heard answering quietly from backstage: "I dunno. Dean Martin is drunk; Sammy Davis hadda go to da temple; Peter Lawford's out campaigning for his brother-in-law."

At the Sands, in the midst of chaos and pure corn—Sinatra beating a bass drum that advertises his L.A. beanery, or Dean Martin drinking Scotch from an ice bucket—Joey can still be funny. When Sammy Davis swings into "She'd Live in a Tent," Joey worriedly pretends to detect an Arab influence, announces: "Jewish people don't live in tents. We don't even smoke Camels." When Senator Jack Kennedy caught the show last week, Joey told him, "If you get in, Frank has to be Ambassador to Italy and Sammy to Israel. I don't want too much for myself—just don't let me get drafted again." Turning to the medical profession, he muses: "My doctor is wonderful. Once, in 1955, when I couldn't afford an operation, he touched up the X rays."

Joey's quips are delivered with a warmth that never wounds. Even the self-protective Sinatra loves them . . . the nightly "meetings," says

Dean, Sammy, Peter, Frank, and Joey cutting loose (Courtesy Sands Hotel Collection, University of Nevada, Las Vegas Library)

Frank in a masterfully mixed metaphor, *"could not have come off without the Speaker of the House—Joey Bishop, the hub of the big wheel."*

The shows electrified Vegas and ignited the imagination of a country just waking up from its Eisenhower-era slumber. Everyone wanted a piece of the on-stage action, to be somehow associated with this phenomenon. It wasn't unusual to see Milton Berle, Red Skelton, or Bob Hope jump up on stage to banter with the Pack; Lucille Ball, Jack Benny, and Kirk Douglas were some of the celebrities who took in the shows, described by *Playboy* writer Robert Legare as "gasping brilliance." And Joey took center stage.

"One of the things I remember about Joey was that he took risks," said Henry Silva, who co-starred in *Ocean's 11* as Roger Corneal and never missed a Summit show. "One night they're doing the show, and Frank was gonna come out. So Joey says, 'Wait a minute, let's give a little breathing room to this member of the Mafia.' Everybody knew about [Sinatra's connections] but no one talked about it. And Frank fell apart laughing. Joey was a ballsy guy. He was funny and daring and there was no other comic like him. He risked it with Frank and said audacious things, but Frank loved anybody who had balls. He wanted to be respected, but he liked people who were kind of on the edge."

Joey's independent streak wasn't just stage shtick. He loved Sinatra and loved being part of The Rat Pack, but he refused to be bullied by anyone. It was a stubborn personality trait picked up on by Gehman when penning *Sinatra and His Rat Pack*, the best-written source for capturing those heady days in Las Vegas.

Bishop is the only member of Sinatra's gang who can tell The Leader what to do with himself and not only get away with it but actually, incredibly enough, become more firmly entrenched in favor. While they were making Ocean's 11, *Sinatra became nettled with the proprietor of a certain Las Vegas club. He gave orders that none of his friends were to go there. According to a Las Vegas press agent friend of mine, Bishop was the only one who went. Bishop, when I spoke to him in April of this year, denied the story emphatically; or, more specifically, he said he had never heard it.*

Yet the fact that the story was circulated is in some ways illustrative of the position Bishop holds in The Rat Pack. He is in it, but not quite of it; and, strangely enough, despite his independence, he holds the other members together—especially when they are performing.

Joey might have had his independent streak, but he wasn't about to bad-mouth Sinatra in any forum. He had seen what had happened to Sammy Davis Jr. after his infamous Chicago radio interview, and he always made sure to sing Frank's praises in public whenever he was asked about The Leader.

"Nobody knows all the wonderful things Frank does," Joey told Gehman. "At the time of the Marciano-Walcott fight, Frank was taking me in a party. My old man is a fight bug, a real nut. I asked Frank, 'Frank, could I give my ticket to my father?' He said, 'No.' Then I found out that he gave his ticket to my old man. He got in by walking in with Walcott's managers, and he had a much worse seat due to that.

"He was working in Miami once when I was too, but in different places. My wife wanted to go and see him. He was sold out, as always. He heard she wanted to come and he had a seat put on the stage for her. When Mildred Bailey, the singer, passed away, Frank paid a lot of her hospital and funeral bills—so I heard. He keeps Red Norvo—he was Mildred's husband for a while—working all the time.

"We did that inaugural ball in Washington, you know. Some of us wished we had pictures of ourselves doing it, it's a thing to remember. My wife just called me and said Frank had sent home an album bound in leather full of those pictures. Same thing when we were doing *Ocean's 11*. He gave all of us in the cast a leather script holder. The consideration he has for the guys he works with goes far beyond that.

"We were shooting at Warner's. Every day, everybody who worked that day got invited to his dressing room for lunch, not a commissary lunch, one he sent out for. One day there was a fellow who had maybe one, maybe two lines to say. He didn't come to the lunch. Maybe he thought Frank wouldn't want him, his part was so small. Frank sent a car to pick him up and bring him there."

Like Bogie's Rat Pack, Sinatra's Rat Pack were politically incorrect boozers (except for teetotaling Joey). And they had their own set of rules—namely that there *were* no rules, except to have a good time, to try to keep up with Frank (who seemingly never slept) and to adhere to the Pack's strict dress code (suits by Sy Devore—no exceptions allowed).

They were, at first, dubbed "The Clan," a term that didn't stick long, obviously out of respect for Sammy and Joey—a black man and a Jew. Sinatra didn't care much for the resurrected "Rat Pack" sobriquet, either. It was a label affixed to the guys once they began their nightly performances, but at least it wasn't offensive to Sammy. Yet neither Frank, Dean, Peter, nor even Joey thought it hurtful to Sammy that, night after night, they would joke about his skin color, eliciting Sammy's forced laughter (no one laughed *that* hard). "Keep smiling so they can see you, Smokey," Frank would say, or "Hurry up, Sam, the watermelon's gettin' warm."

Joey, who wrote the majority of The Pack's stage show, took pride in claiming authorship of the "gag" in which Dean would pick Sammy up, carry him over to the microphone and announce: "I'd like to thank the NAACP for giving me this award."

But in that time, in that atmosphere, it worked. By 1960 standards The Rat Pack's stage patter was a sign of the times. The Civil Rights Movement was in its infancy and was still several years away. When Frank, Dean, Sammy, Peter, and Joey arrived in Las Vegas the city wasn't even integrated. Sammy and other black performers were welcomed to play the Sands, Desert Inn, or Flamingo any time. But they couldn't stay in those hotels once the show ended and were forced to leave through a back entrance. The Rat Pack's crowning achievement, such as it was, was the integration of Las Vegas. Sinatra demanded that Sammy be allowed to stay in The Sands, and he got his way. No matter that Frank's nickname for Sammy was "Smokey" (because he smoked, according to Sinatra)—he was a member of The Pack, and no one, NO ONE, fucked with any of Frank's friends.

"If you reach stardom you've got to be true to yourself," Joey said at the time. "Frank is honest—that's for sure. He and the boys do things not for their effect on people but because they believe in them all the way. Am I a full-fledged member? No, I'm more of a mascot, but even the mascot gets to carry the ball, too."

Hindsight is 20/20, of course, and no one was paying attention to sociology during the filming of *Ocean's 11*. The movie and the Copa Room shows were all about fun—and there certainly was plenty of that going on.

"It was so much fun and we had all these chicks with us—goddammit, the place was crawling with the most gorgeous girls you could possibly imagine," said Henry Silva. "These women were not eye candy, they were bedtime candy. These gorgeous girls would stick their key in your pocket and say, 'Come on up to room whatever, I'll be there, I'll be bathed, I'll take care of you, make love to you like you've never been made love to before.' You could have two or three girls at the same time.

"It was highly sexual but there was no meanness, no control. It was just a bunch of guys with a tremendous amount of freedom of thought, movement, emotion . . . it was a great time."

Somehow, the movie got made. Sinatra treated *Ocean's 11* as a daytime diversion, something to keep the party going once the sun came up and he caught a few hours of sleep. He refused to do multiple takes and had his hand in every aspect of the movie; director Lewis Milestone was little more than a traffic cop, making sure the guys hit their marks. After the day's filming was completed—no one worked more than three hours a day—Frank, Dean, Sammy, Peter, and Joey repaired to The Sands steam room around 6 o'clock for some rest and relaxation, wearing the terrycloth robes Sinatra had given them with their nicknames emblazoned on the back: The Leader (Frank), The Dago (Dean), Smokey (Sammy), Charlie the Seal (Peter, for his hacking cough), and The Needler (Joey).

"It was the greatest time of my life," Joey said. "There was only one bad thing about it, though. I was in the first scene to be shot in the mornings while everyone else slept in. I remember that billing in those days was 'Four Kings and a Joker.'"

"They all had a wonderful, childlike energy," Silva said. "You could take their chronological age and put that aside. Besides all the sexual energy and testosterone, there was a real kind of trust. There was something very young about it. The excitement of *Ocean's 11* was the excitement of a bunch of guys who never finished high school and fought for what they wanted."

"They were at the top of their game, the top of their pleasure period. I mean, they loved Vegas," said Angie Dickinson, who had a small role in *Ocean's 11*.

"They were larger than life all the time. That was no act," she said. "I don't think they ever got tired. First of all, it was an easy shoot and Frank liked 'French hours.' He liked the 11 to 7, rather than the 6 or 7 A.M. to 5 P.M. hours, so they didn't have to get up early. They could go to work on the set, come back, shower, and just kind of relax and were then ready to go on stage. I think that was where they partied. As a matter of fact, I don't think they partied much after."

Ocean's 11 wrapped the Vegas end of production in mid-February after a twenty-five-day shooting schedule (Sinatra tallied a scant nine

"The Joker" cracks up his pals. (Courtesy Sands Hotel Collection, University of Nevada, Las Vegas Library)

days on the set). The Summit then moved to The Fontainbleu in Miami for a week ($17.50 for drinks, dinner and cover charge to see the show). The Summit shows in The Fontainbleau didn't differ much from their Vegas counterparts. Joey, as he had done in The Copa Room, opened the show. "What's Frank doing?" a voice asked from the darkened stage. "We lost him," Joey replied. "He went down to the beach this morning and a dog ran off with him. Not a dog, bow-wow, but a dog. A broad." When the lights came up, Joey sauntered on stage. "Some time I want to work in a room where there's a Jewish orchestra and *Spanish* people are dancing." He broke the place up. Soon thereafter Frank and Dean walked on stage, looked at each other, shrugged, and walked off. "Son of a gun," Joey said. "Italian penguins."

Richard Gehman, writing about the Fontainbleau shows in *Sinatra and His Rat Pack,* noted that the off-color jokes and ethnic slurs—ostensibly said in jest—began to make the Miami crowd a bit uncomfortable.

The jovial spirit of the five men working together was such that they could use off-color jokes—"blue" material—and even jokes about minorities and get away with them, although as the evening went on I began to feel that perhaps at times they went too far in their references to each other's ancestry and religion. When Peter Lawford said he wanted to dance with Sammy, the latter said:

"You want to dance with me? Do you realize I happen to be the greatest Jewish Mau-Mau dancer of all time?"

"I'm not prejudiced," Lawford said.

"I know your kind—you'll dance with me but you won't go to school with me," Davis said.

After the dance, Bishop, referring to Martin and Sinatra, said to the two of them, "You guys better get off—the Italian natives are getting restless." Some people in the audience also must have felt restless, for toward the end the laughs at the broad jokes became less enthusiastic.

Most of the truly funny lines were Bishop's. When Martin twitted Sinatra about his new tuxedo, Sinatra said, "Why do you think I put this on?" and Bishop interrupted, "What the hell, if you're gonna look dead, dress dead."

Sinatra began to sing 'What Is This Thing Called Love?' "Boy," said Bishop, "if you don't know . . ."

*Beginning to sing 'She's Funny That Way,' Sinatra said, "Not
much to look at, nothing to see . . ." Bishop said, "You can say that
again, Frank. If you stand sideways, they'll mark you absent."*

*Sinatra said to Bishop, "You got a fairy godmother?" "No," Bishop
said, "but we got an uncle we keep a close eye on."*

In March, Sinatra and most of the *Ocean's 11* cast were required
in Los Angeles for five more weeks of shooting. Joey, reaching back
into his past, managed to snare a small role for his old comedy partner, Rummy Bishop.

*Joey, Frank, Nancy Sinatra, and Sammy were on hand to welcome home Elvis Presley
on* The Frank Sinatra Timex Show—*Presley's first TV appearance after being discharged from the Army. Peter Lawford also put in an appearance. (Courtesy ABC
Photography Archives)*

"Joey did a lot for me," Rummy said. "I was living in Pittsburgh at the time he was doing *Ocean's 11*, and Joey wanted me to come out to Los Angeles. I happened to be on the set when they were shooting the scene around the pool table and Joey walked toward me with the director, who says to me, 'Would you mind reading this?' So I read it like I was reading a label from a bottle, and Joey comes back and says to me, 'You schmuck! The guy wanted you to read it like you were reading the lines!' I said I didn't know it was an audition . . . anyway I got the part and I'm in the scene after the robbery is pulled—it's George Raft's cameo scene where all the club owners are sitting around the table. I play Mr. Gillette.

"One part led to another, and from there I went on to do *77 Sunset Strip* and *The Alaskan* with Roger Moore."

That same month, Frank, Joey, Sammy, and Peter flew back to The Fontainbleau to tape Sinatra's *Welcome Home, Elvis* TV special, part of *The Frank Sinatra–Timex Show* marking Elvis Presley's first national appearance since being discharged from the Army. ABC paid Presley $125,000 for his six minutes on the special—a record sum at the time but well worth the "get" for which everyone was clamoring.

"We're in Miami doing our act at The Fountainbleau, Frank, Dean, Sammy, and the rest," Joey said. "He's doing the television show from there with Presley. He asked me to do it. I said, 'I'd like to do it but I have to have my price.' 'What's your price?' he asked me. 'Seventy-five hundred,' I said. 'I can't give you seventy-five hundred, he said, 'you get eighty-five hundred.' These are the things Frank does that nobody ever hears about."

Joey provided the comic relief during the opening, in which he, Frank, Sammy, Nancy Sinatra, and others surround Presley, wearing his Army uniform, to sing "It's Nice to Go Traveling."

"Where the heck are his sideburns?!" Joey yelled, to which Presley shouted back, "In Germany!"

Most of Joey's chores on the special involved his reading lame, scripted dialogue as he "joked" with Sinatra:

You know I had the feeling all along that Elvis was gonna re-enlist. Some very important people were hoping that he'd stay in. People like Fabian, Ricky Nelson, Tab Hunter . . .

I'll tell you one thing, Frank, you're a pretty good loser. I mean throwing this homecoming must have set you back a few bucks . . . they tell me that for what it's costing you for Presley you could have presented World War II in person . . .

Joey managed to get off a few zingers ("What are they all screaming about?" he asked Sinatra of the females in the audience. "Are the rates too high in Florida?") He also mistakenly referred to Sinatra as, "exhausted one," instead of "exalted one" and told Sinatra, "One mistake you're entitled to" when Frank blew a line.

Sammy did some impressions (Nat King Cole, Cary Grant) and joined Peter in a soft-shoe number. At one point, all four Rat Packers (Dean was elsewhere) shared the stage. The special snared nearly 42 percent of the viewing audience when it premiered in May—huge numbers, especially for ABC, which didn't have the affiliate strength of powerhouse competitors CBS and NBC. *Welcome Home, Elvis* would prove to be Presley's last TV appearance until his "comeback" special in 1968.

For Joey, though, the *Welcome Home, Elvis* special marked his return to television, where he hadn't appeared at all while filming *Ocean's 11*. That quickly changed once *Ocean's 11* wrapped production. Joey did a few *What's My Line?* shows on CBS in the spring of 1960 and filmed a fleeting cameo in the gangster movie *Pepe*, where he uttered his now-famous catchphrase, "Son of a gun!" ("The guy came up to me and said he'd pay me a thousand bucks a word for the movie job," he said. "It turned out that all I had to say was one word . . . and the guy insisted on the hyphens.")

But television was Joey's meat-and-potatoes. Now, with the boost from *Ocean's 11*—which wouldn't open until August but was already generating advance buzz—the possibilities seemed endless.

And what better way to get back into television than to pick a fight with Ed Sullivan, who ruled Sunday nights on CBS? Sullivan's public feuds were legendary, among them Walter Winchell, Jack Paar, and Steve Allen. Joey joined the club when he told *New York Post* TV columnist Bob Williams that he had rejected Sullivan's offer of ten guest shots at $8,500 a pop.

"You're booked for six or seven minutes, then suddenly you're cut to six or five," Joey said. "Then, just when you're ready to go on, you're cut to four."

Joey's comments rankled Sullivan, who fired back four days later.

"This is completely untrue," he told Williams. "Instead of relishing his success, with which all of show business is delighted, Bishop is getting too big for his breeches. He suddenly thinks he wrote the book. It makes a big man out of him to the hambones.

"I don't think we should be maligned by a guy like this who, because of Sinatra's support, suddenly got hot," Sullivan said. "We played golf together, and I never offered him a damn thing. What I resent is this guy stepping in as a great big man. Some guys start feeling their oats and decide they're going to dictate to TV shows."

Joey stuck to his guns, calling Sullivan "a wonderful man" but insisting that he was offered the deal. "What I was trying to say was that even a couple of years ago, when I really needed the money, I refused to go on variety shows unless I was integrated into the program," he told Williams.

"I decided it was just senseless to go on a program where everyone was merely interested in their show. Those shows go on forever but all of a sudden the performer is in oblivion."

Sullivan was having none of it, recalling Joey's first appearance on *The Ed Sullivan Show* four years earlier.

"That was his eighth appearance on the show. He didn't have any complaint then," Sullivan said. "He has never made any complaint to me since. It certainly has taken him a long time to get angry."

"I will refresh Ed's memory for him," Joey shot back. "I explained to him then that I just didn't want to do stand-up spots anymore. Certain comedians have certain attitudes, which can only be established in a certain amount of time. When they're victimized they can't convey the attitude they're trying to convey.

"Ed's a wonderful man," Joey said. "But he's interested in *The Ed Sullivan Show*. I'm interested in Joey Bishop's career."

Sullivan had the final word. "Bishop makes it sound as if we don't know what we're doing," he said. "We've been around a long time so we must know something. If Sam Levenson, Shelley Berman, Bob Newhart, Jack Carter, Wayne and Shuster, Ricky Layne, and Velvel and other comics can take the time allotted to them on our show and kill audiences, it's a strong indication that what Bishop is saying is not true."

If Joey had shot himself in the foot vis-à-vis Sullivan, he didn't seem to care. He had plenty of TV work coming down the pike, including a starring role in a CBS adaptation of *Heaven Can Wait* and an October appearance on *The Jack Benny Show*, guest-starring with his idol. As far as movies, there would be more Rat Pack frolics under the "five-year plan" envisioned by Sinatra for Dean, Sammy, Peter, and Joey.

7

The Arch Bishop

In the meantime, Danny Thomas had come calling about a possible television series. Thomas' series, *Make Room for Daddy*, had been a hit since premiering in 1953, and Thomas had established a burgeoning TV empire under his Danny Thomas Productions banner, which was gaining a reputation as "The Supermarket of Sitcoms" with shows like *The Dick Van Dyke Show* and *The Real McCoys*. In February 1960, while Joey was filming *Ocean's 11* in Las Vegas, Thomas had featured Joey's *Onionhead* co-star, Andy Griffith, in an episode of *Make Room for Daddy*. That episode revolved around Danny Williams (Thomas) encountering country-bumpkin sheriff Andy Taylor in the sleepy town of Mayberry, North Carolina. The episode went over well, and now Thomas was spinning Griffith off into his own show, *The Andy Griffith Show*, which was slated to debut in September on CBS.

Thomas had been a fan of Joey's dating back to that 1946 policemen's benefit at Madison Square Garden. Now, Thomas envisioned for Joey a scenario similar to Griffith's situation, in which Joey would guest-star on *Make Room for Daddy*. Joey's guest-starring episode would be considered a pilot for a possible series. If the episode was a success, Thomas would spin Joey off into his own series. Joey was intrigued by the possibility.

He wasn't intrigued, however, when Vice President Richard Nixon's office called, asking Joey if he would perform at the Republican National Convention in Chicago. Joey had never openly expressed any political affiliations, and didn't do so now.

The Rat Pack stumps for JFK. (Courtesy Sands Hotel Collection, University of Nevada, Las Vegas Library)

But he didn't really need to: his Rat Pack association with Sinatra and the "Brother-in-Lawford" guaranteed Joey Bishop's loyalty to Senator John F. Kennedy, who was considered the underdog in his 1960 battle with Nixon for the White House.

"I had a call from the White House. Nixon's secretary called to invite me to perform at the convention next week," Joey told columnist Maria Torre. "I didn't know what to do. I thanked the secretary and the Vice President for thinking of me, but I said I was too busy to go. After all, should Nixon lose, I'd be out politically, out professionally.

"Actually, I'm a Kennedy man," Joey said. "Have been since that nightclub encounter when Kennedy told me he's been a fan of mine for years."

Joey knew any association with Nixon would be professional suicide, at least as it pertained to his friendship with Sinatra and The Rat Pack, who were now out beating the drum for Kennedy. Sinatra had redubbed his buddies "The Jack Pack," had, at JFK's request, reworked the Sammy Cahn/Jimmy Van Heusen song "High Hopes" into a pro-Kennedy ditty ("Everyone wants to back Jack/Jack is on the right track"), and had even convinced actress Janet Leigh to hold a "Key Women for Kennedy Tea."

Joey knew what he was up against. Had he agreed to perform for Nixon it would have almost certainly guaranteed his banishment from the Rat Pack, and from their next stop: the Democratic National Convention in Los Angeles, where Frank, Dean, Sammy, Peter, and Joey sang the national anthem (to a chorus of boos aimed at Sammy from the Alabama and Mississippi delegations).

And there were still the publicity commitments for *Ocean's 11* and the carnival-like atmosphere surrounding the movie's premiere. The city of Las Vegas went all out for the August 3rd event, covering the "Welcome to Las Vegas" sign with an *Ocean's 11* banner and hosting a Summit reunion (Frank, Dean, Sammy, Peter, and Joey) with a live show in front of The Freemont Theatre. Joey emceed the event—interviewing his Rat Pack buddies and guest star George Raft—then flew off to Chicago with Sylvia and Larry. He was booked for a summer-theater run at the Highland Park Playhouse in his first legitimate stage appearance, co-starring in *Who Was That Lady?* ("Just a change of pace," he said. "I still want to be a comic.")

Ocean's 11 opened to generally fair-to-middling reviews. Most critics cited the movie's "inside" jokes, its overall lack of plot and pacing and the cast's seeming to sleepwalk through the picture (no surprise considering the hours Sinatra and company kept during the movie's filming).

"*Ocean's 11* is an odd picture, half seeming to be an insider's joke, a little coterie romp, or charades for Sinatra's friends, and half a reworking in Las Vegas terms of an excellent crime formula,"

August, 1960: Emcee Joey interviews Ocean's 11 *co-stars George Raft and Frank Sinatra at the movie's glitzy Las Vegas premiere on Freemont Street.*

Archer Winsten wrote in *The New York Post*. "The scheme of robbery is sufficiently ingenious, and it photographs well in color, as does most of Las Vegas, and most of the characters.

"If this picture can be parlayed and advertised and publicized into a great success of names and décor, then they've gotten away with real murder. If not, and the public ignores one of the truly empty displays on the movie record, then maybe some of these many talents will be forced to go to work . . . Get a story, fellows, or a horse or something."

"The picture runs over two hours, and almost half of it is devoted to wisecracks exchanged by Mr. Sinatra and his talkative troops, who include Dean Martin, Peter Lawford, Sammy Davis Jr., Richard Conte, and Joey Bishop," wrote *Herald-Tribune* critic Joseph Morgenstern. "Some of the dialogue is funny. Too much of it is Damon Runyon froth with a dash of old Cole Porter champagne. Moreover, the screenplay is full of 'inside' jokes which are mildly amusing at their best and tasteless at their worst." The movie even engendered a short-lived controversy when a group of disabled veterans in Winston-Salem, N.C., blasted *Ocean's 11* as "an attempt to besmirch and ridicule the name of America's veterans."

Joey spent the fall of 1960 playing Vegas and making numerous television appearances, including two spots on *The Jack Benny Show* and as a panelist on *What's My Line?* (where fellow South Philadelphian Bobby Darin was one of that week's mystery guests). He even did a *Person to Person* appearance in December, with he and Sylvia being interviewed in their Englewood home by show host Charles Collingwood. (Sylvia was supposed to greet Collingwood while she was dusting the TV set. Everything went fine in rehearsal, but when Collingwood said, "Hello, Sylvia," on the air she fainted dead away.)

Joey played the Copacabana in November—finally the headliner!—and then flew out to Los Angeles for a TV special called *Happy Talk* with host David Susskind and fellow guests George Burns, Jimmy Durante, Buddy Hackett, and Groucho Marx. In between these commitments, Joey found time to fill in again for Jack Paar. Paar seemed to be growing restless with *The Jack Paar Show* and was continuously butting heads with NBC. The previous February, he had

Domestic bliss: Larry, Sylvia, and Joey at home in Englewood, New Jersey. (Courtesy ABC Photography Archives)

stalked off the show in tears when he was censored by NBC for using the words "water closet" in a joke.

The censors were nowhere to be found, however, when Joey was accorded the ultimate honor by his show-biz brethren in November: a Friar's Club roast in Los Angeles, emceed by caustic comic Jack E. Leonard.

Joey's prominence at that time was unquestionable. The roast, to quote *Variety* columnist Army Archerd, featured "a double-dais of nitery names rarely equaled at a testimonial," including Milton Berle, George Burns, Jack Benny, George Jessel, Henny Youngman, Danny Thomas, Jack Lemmon, Rocky Marciano, and Carol Burnett. Noticeably absent were Frank, Dean, Sammy, and Peter, who were all shooting movies. Nancy Sinatra and Deana Martin (Dean's daughter) were the only links to The Rat Pack who showed up to Joey's roast.

Benny got the evening rolling. "For 18 years I was his idol," he said, turning to Joey, who was seated next to Sylvia. "I remained his idol until three weeks ago when ABC renewed his contract for 52 weeks . . . I appeared on his show for a lousy $260, but when I asked him to appear on my special for a very short spot, he wanted $20,000 . . . Today this guy is his own idol."

George Burns: "You deserve this tribute from all of your friends—I can't wait to be one."

Corbett Monica: "I'm his third-best friend—if I were on earlier I'd have been his best friend."

Jack E. Leonard: "I've heard more laughs for organ music."

Johnny Carson: "Joey Bishop's feuding with Ed Sullivan. It's a clash of personalities. Neither has any. Joey looks like an untipped waiter. Sullivan has the sparkle of the back wall of a handball court."

Finally it was Joey's turn to speak.

"I have a funny feeling that somewhere right now Frank Sinatra is hitting a photographer in the mouth. I'm never going to forget this affair, and when I say I'm not going to forget it, you're fucking right! I'm not going to forget it! I'll have retribution. So hand me the plaque and let's get the hell out of here. I'm a little busy. Forget the damn plaque!"

Earlier that month, John F. Kennedy had been elected president by the slimmest of margins. That was good news for Sinatra, who was already planning JFK's inaugural gala. And where there was Sinatra, there was, inevitably, The Rat Pack. Frank, Dean, Sammy, Peter, and Joey had been vocal in their support of JFK and had worked hard to get him elected as the country's first Catholic president. Now it was the Rat Pack's turn to soak up a little bit of the Camelot glory in Washington, which had been hit hard by a snowstorm just prior to President Kennedy's inauguration. Joey, perhaps, had the biggest honor of them all: He was chosen by Frank to emcee JFK's inaugural gala, much to Kennedy's delight.

Joey, outfitted in tux and tails, kept the celebrity-packed crowd roaring from the get-go (Larry had a plum seat next to Tony Curtis). Looking up at JFK and Jackie Kennedy, Joey exclaimed, "I told you I'd get you a good seat. And you were so worried!" "I was emceeing JFK's inaugural and my opening line was, "Mr. President, now that you've been elected, can you tell me how I get that sticker off my bumper?'" Joey said. "I don't know where that came from."

Sinatra performed a few songs and micro-managed the evening down to the last detail. Milton Berle, Nat King Cole, Red Skelton, Juliet Prowse, and a myriad of others entertained the president-elect. Peter, the "Brother-in-Lawford," was there, of course, but Dean and Sammy were noticeably absent. Dean, who was shooting a movie, had absolutely no interest in JFK or politics and couldn't be bothered. It was a different story for Sammy. After working his ass off for JFK's campaign, Sammy had been banned from the inauguration ceremonies by Kennedy patriarch Joseph P. Kennedy, who feared Sammy's interracial marriage to Swedish starlet May Britt would send "the wrong message" to America. Now, Sammy was too pissed off and wounded to attend the gala. He would never again voice his support for JFK.

Joey parlayed his prominence at President Kennedy's inaugural gala into a hosting appearance later that spring at the White House Correspondents' Dinner featuring the new president. Scheduled host Danny Thomas was unable to attend, and Joey was called in as a last-minute replacement. He brought along old pal Rummy Bishop, now doing a solo act, as his guest.

"Joey called me and said, 'Look, I got an idea,' Rummy said. "'Danny Thomas can't make it, so I'm going to introduce you by saying, 'If you wanna see a nose, I'm gonna have you meet a real nose. Danny Thomas has got nothing on this guy!' But he never did it in the show.

"I was sitting at a table with Adlai Stevenson and Toots Shor. I remember Stevenson had a hearing problem, and after every one of Joey's jokes, he'd lean over and say, 'What was that he said?' So I went backstage and told that to Joey. So the next time Joey tells a joke, he turns to Stevenson and says, 'If you wanna know what I just said, ask me. What are you asking that guy for?'"

Joey also broke 'em up during the show when two stagehands began loudly moving a piano on stage. Turning around quickly, Joey said, "Don't tell me HE'S back again!"

"Bishop: Show-Biz's No. 1 Sub," Hollywood columnist Sheila Graham dubbed Joey soon thereafter. But that all changed in May 1961 when Joey was tapped to host the New York portion of the Emmy Awards while Dick Powell hosted in Hollywood. In those days, the Emmys were a bi-coastal affair, with awards presented simultaneously in Los Angeles and New York.

"This is the first time I haven't substituted for someone," Joey said. "No one got ill. No one got mad. They wanted me.

"I've pitched in for Jack Paar when he vacationed. I've been a panel member for the regulars on *What's My Line?* I substituted for Danny Thomas at the White House Correspondents' Dinner Show. Just recently Sir Cedric Hardwicke couldn't make it as a guest speaker for the Executives' Club of Chicago. They put in a rush call for me and I obliged."

The Emmy Awards went off without a hitch, although one awkward moment occurred when Barbara Stanwyck ripped her gown while rushing up to accept a lifetime achievement award. Stanwyck fumbled around while someone helped her put a coat over her evening gown. "The guy who helped Barbara Stanwyck with her coat was on camera longer than I was!" Joey quipped.

Soon thereafter Joey received a call from Sinatra. The Rat Pack was congregating in the desolate town of Kanab, Utah, that summer for their second movie, *Sergeants 3*, a comic treatment of *Gunga Din* directed by John Sturges. It was originally titled *Soldiers Three* but that was later changed when MGM threatened legal action (it had used *Soldiers Three* for a 1953 release).

Joey's role in *Sergeants 3*, as Roger Boswell, wasn't much bigger than Mushy O'Connors had been in *Ocean's 11*. Frank, Dean, Sammy, and Peter carried the on-screen load in *Sergeants 3*. ("Load" being a good word to describe Lawford. As Shawn Levy points out in his book, *Rat Pack Confidential,* Peter had gained about 30 pounds before arriving in Kanab.)

Joey as courtly Roger Boswell in the second Rat Pack movie, Sergeants Three. *(Courtesy The Kobal Collection)*

"Before the picture started, Frank says to me, 'Can you ride a horse?'" Joey said. "I said, 'I never been on a horse in my life.' He says, 'Learn to ride 'cause you're the sergeant in charge, you're going to be leading us. Get a wrangler. Hire the best guy you can get.' So for two months, religiously—I mean I couldn't walk, my back was hurting, everything—I practice, stopping the horse dead, around barrels, going into a full gallop from a dead start.

"This is for two months. Finally, I get the script and I go through it. On page 117 I am with a horse but I'm walking it. I'm holding the reins. And that's my only connection with a horse."

There also wasn't much to do in Kanab, as Sonny King discovered when he flew out to the location. Joey had helped to get Sonny, Rummy Bishop, and Mel Bishop small roles in the movie.

"I came in two days later to be on the set of *Sergeants 3*, and I called Joey up to ask what kind of clothes to bring to Kanab," King said. "I also asked Joey what kind of action was happening there. He says, 'Listen, Sonny, when you get off the plane, go directly to the Dairy Queen and order a double scoop of ice cream. And lick it slow—because after that there's absolutely nothing to do.'"

Dean, Joey, and Frank get serious in Sergeants 3 *(1961). (The Kobal Collection)*

That was Joey's private view of Kanab. Publicly, he kept up an enthusiastic (for him) front, not wanting to offend the good people of Utah. Remaining inoffensive was the same rationale he had used before, as part of the "everyman" image Joey worked so hard to perpetuate. He had already told Frank and Dean that he felt uncomfortable when they referred to each other as "dago" and that he would refuse to go on stage with them if they continued using the word (they stopped). Appearing on stage with Jack Benny, Joey had declined to use certain jokes he felt would "hurt" Benny and, by association, Joey's on-stage appeal as someone who didn't offend anyone.

So when Joey arrived in Kanab, he was greeted by a local press agent, who wanted to stir up some publicity for the movie. The press agent's idea was that he would circulate a story to the press that Dean had sent Joey a postcard from Kanab—and that Joey had immediately sent a CARE package to Dean (because the town was so dull). Joey killed the idea immediately. "What will the people of Kanab think?" he told the deflated press agent.

Sergeants 3 opened to the same types of reviews that had greeted *Ocean's 11:* not great, not bad, but somewhere in between, with critics praising the movie's laid-back atmosphere but questioning its use of "inside" references.

"Mr. Sinatra, Dean Martin, Peter Lawford, Sammy Davis Jr., and Joey Bishop who joined forces, if not all their talents, to rob all the money of a modern Nevada gambling town in *Ocean's 11,* give the strange impression in *Sergeants 3* of having never left a Las Vegas nightclub," wrote *New York Times* critic A. H. Weiler.

"Mr. Sinatra, as the top-kick and brains of the outfit, is, except for brief spells of animation, casual in the extreme, as is Peter Lawford, the suave and educated member of the trio. As the zany sergeant, Dean Martin is relaxed, most of the way, to the point of lethargy. Sammy Davis Jr. as a freed slave . . . is spirited, if not entirely convincing. Ruta Lee, as Mr. Lawford's fiancee, is merely decorative. And Joey Bishop, as a straight-laced sergeant major, is, except for a mildly comic drinking bout, as stony-faced as any Sioux."

But what *Sergeants 3* lacked in critical admiration it more than compensated for in star power—namely, the power of the Rat Pack to promote the movie. Frank, Dean, and Joey (no Sammy or Peter) did just that in the fall of 1961. Sinatra, as usual, was headlining at The Sands, with Joey and Dean waiting (unbilled) in the wings. Sinatra walked out and announced to the audience that he had a sore throat. What follows is typical Rat Pack silliness.

Frank: I have been here since June and I'm pleased to come back. This is what you call the occupational hazard here in Vegas. It happens to almost every performer for maybe one day or two days and then it goes away. I've had it for three years now and it won't leave me. Today I was visited by six doctors. They brought a guy from San Francisco, Los Angeles, Hawaii. A small Japanese doctor came in and we did a scene from Pearl Harbor. I was walking to work for the first show, and I passed a busboy who said [switches to Japanese accent] 'How do you feel Mr. Sinatra?' I said I don't feel so good. He said why don't you loosen your tie? So now I talk like this. I'd like to join you in a drink but I find a little tea and honey is better for me because it softens all of the throat.

(Joey appears on stage to thunderous applause, bearing a teacup.)

Frank: I know it's a joke that you brought the tea out, Joey. I'm sorry that you came to visit me and I've got a little problem.

Joey: I didn't come to visit you Frank. You put in a phone call you got the first plane.

Frank: Would you like to help me out while you're up here, maybe sing a song?

Joey: Would you let me sing? I thought what would be nice, you know, like the kids do on the Dick Clark show. Stars come on and they mouth it, see, and then somebody sings it. So I'll sing it off-stage if you'll mouth it that way. You'll have another respite and it'll give you a chance to come back to your own voice again.

Frank: Good idea. What'll we do?

Joey: How about "Bye Bye Blackbird"?

Frank: Sammy Davis doesn't like that word . . .

Joey: Well, you wanna try "Bye Bye Bluebird"?

Frank: I think he's got a little of that in him, too.

Joey: He's [Sammy] in Israel now, explaining himself to Ben Gurion.

Frank: Okay, I'll mouth it, you sing it, okay? Whenever you're ready, I'll give you the signal.

Joey: The stuff you've been getting by with for years.

Frank: Ready, Joey?

(Dean appears on stage, again to thunderous applause. He begins singing.)

Dean (to Joey): Have you ever seen a jujitsu?

Joey: There they are, folks, Haig and Haig, two Italian penguins. I have to leave now, I think I'm wanted in surgery. Settle down folks please, The Leader wants to talk.

Frank: Can I go lie down for 30 seconds?

Joey: Just give him a chance to recuperate. Dean, the audience is out *here*.

Dean: They keep moving 'em around!

Joey: Hold it down, folks. Frank's substitute will now sing. And don't forget when he's through, no whistling, just applause.

Joey: What song you gonna sing, Dean?

Dean: "Oh, Wonderful."

Joey: Good. Do you guys know "Oh, Wonderful?" In the key of L. Hold it down, folks, Dean's gonna sing. Frank, put that plane down! What's the song, Dean? I'll announce it while you talk it over with the guys. You can at least say excuse me.

Dean (to Frank): You hit it right on the wall, did you baby? Hey, how's your throat now?

Joey (to Frank): He doesn't know he didn't sing, don't say nothing. [To audience]: Wait 'till he finds out it's Frank's club he's working. See how these Italians congregate? I wish Sammy was here. They've got me outnumbered again. You guys gonna sing or you gonna play?

Dean: You mind if I make a toast?

Joey: It's a new game—I hold the mike and he talks. Here we are folks, McCarthy and Bergen. I'll stand here until you think of it. Here we are folks, *Lost Weekend* and me . . .

Dean: I kissed a brown-eyed aging cow who gave me milk and cheese. Now I'm lying on my back with hoof-and-mouth disease.

Joey: Good. Jump through that. Maybe you ought to propose another toast. Do the one about the queen, I love that one.

Dean: Oh, that's fun.

Joey: Good, a lotta people think we can't ad-lib.

Dean: Here's to Madam Lepescue who came to King Carol's rescue. It's a wonderful thing to be under a king, can you do that in a democracy I ask you?

Joey: Could you hold the band down?

Dean: I'm gonna sing "Where or When" from the picture . . .

Joey: That wasn't bad, four out of 600 [people clapping]. Dean Martin doing "Where or When." Take it away, Dean!

Dean: Incidentally, I have a sore throat. I've been here overnight, must be the air conditioning in these rooms. Mind telling me how to turn off that air conditioning? There's no way. They keep the butter in my room. I woke up this morning, snow on my bed. I didn't mind that, they sent in some big dog, bottle around its neck. She left at 8:30 . . . So we're gonna do a little song here, hope you enjoy it. This is "Where or When" from that wonderful picture, *Spiral Staircase.*

(Dean starts to sing.)

Joey (to Dean): Say, you did good.

Frank (comes back on stage): Did you hear about the two ladies who got on a drunk and he couldn't get them off?

Joey: Another reason you don't have a television show! Folks, Frank and Dean will now drink two choruses.

Frank: Tell 'em about our picture, Joe.

Joey: Oh, we have a wonderful motion picture, we hope you'll see it. It's called *Sergeants 3* and it stars Frank Sinatra, Dean Martin, Sammy Davis Jr., Peter Lawford, and myself. Can I tell them the plot?

Frank: Yeah.

Joey: See how quick a guy thinks? No, lotta guys you turn around they're idiots. What do you think? Not Frank, God bless him, in one second he said without thinking, "Yeah."

Frank: You can tell them the plot of the picture, we'll give you a writer credit, go ahead.

Joey: Am I not the hero in the picture?

Frank: Yes you are.

Joey: Don't light any flames near you, Dean.

Dean: I drank so much last night my hair hurt.

Joey: I didn't know you had a rabbit. [To the audience, who applauds loudly] Please don't make me a hit when I'm not getting paid. It's a great motion picture, because I turn out to be the hero, because Frank and Dean and Peter Lawford are captured by the Indian chief and he holds them for ransom and he wants firewater, booze, you know, but I outsmart him, I bring him bottles of tea, and he doesn't know it, and that's how I kill him. Because the next morning he's found dead in his own tea pee. But you'll see the picture. . . . Can't the three of us do a duet?

Frank: You wanna join us for a duet?

Dean: Oh, I missed *Highway Patrol* again.

Joey: I can get in here someplace, you'll point to me. Wait till you hear my voice, I hit some notes—only Jewish dogs can hear me.

Frank (starts to sing): "When you're smiling, the whole world smiles with you . . ."

Joey (starts to sing—badly): "When you're crying . . ." I know the words shut your big mouth! I sang one chorus with you guys and I got a hangover! Don't holler fire lady, I'm singing!

(Joey finishes out the song with Frank and Dean.)

Frank: Joey Bishop, Dean Martin. Marvelous people!

Danny Thomas, Joey, and an exasperated Joe Flynn on "Everything Happens to Me," the episode of The Danny Thomas Show that launched Joey's sitcom career. (Courtesy CBS Photo Archive)

Make Room for Joey

I n the spring of 1961 Joey had played a deflated, stony-faced press agent in an episode of *The Danny Thomas Show* that would (hopefully) serve as a pilot for Joey's own series. After moving to CBS in 1957, Thomas' show had undergone a name change from *Make Room for Daddy* to its more banal title.

In the pilot episode, titled "Everything Happens to Me," Joey played Joey Barnes, a nervous Hollywood press agent in charge of a TV spectacular starring Danny Williams (Thomas). On the way from New York to Los Angeles, Danny accidentally mistakes a sleeping pill for an aspirin, and arrives in Los Angeles extremely groggy and out of sorts.

Danny's situation is exacerbated by Joey, who has messed up Danny's hotel reservations and is forced to take the comic back to his house to sleep off the effects of the pill. Danny spends a tough night on Joey's couch and is exposed to Joey's annoying family (mom, dad, and two sisters, one played by Thomas' daughter, Marlo Thomas). Danny figures the experience could be comic fodder for his performance on the TV special. Joey, however, doesn't like the idea of Danny poking fun at his family and convinces Danny to tell the sleeping-pill story instead.

Thomas, who liked what he saw of the episode and of the show's ratings, decided to spin the "Everything Happens to Me" episode off into *The Joey Bishop Show*. With any luck, Danny Thomas Productions would have the same success that it was enjoying with *The Andy Griffith Show*, which was now a bona fide hit entering its second season on CBS.

Danny Thomas Productions sold *The Joey Bishop Show* to NBC, which would air the show in black-and-white. Joey and Sylvia still owned the house in Englewood and were reluctant to take Larry, now 14, out of school (Larry had been valedictorian of his 6th-grade class and was continuing to excel). Joey decided to rent a place in Beverly Hills, see how the show progressed and take it from there. If the show took off, he could always sell the place in Englewood and move Sylvia and Larry out to California. "This will take me away from my family, but I'll probably do it for a couple of years," he said. "It's my chance for real financial security for us." At any rate, Sylvia and Larry would spend the summer with Joey, who was scheduled to begin shooting *The Joey Bishop Show* in July after wrapping *Sergeants 3* in Kanab.

Joey approached his new undertaking with some trepidation. *The Joey Bishop Show* was no *Ocean's 11* or *Sergeants 3*, no supporting role in which Frank, Dean, Sammy, and Peter shouldered the burden. They weren't going to be around now; the success or failure of *The Joey Bishop Show* would rest squarely on Joey's shoulders. And the pressure to produce a hit was intensified by the fact that Joey owned 25 percent of the show—and that he was being paid the princely sum of $3,500 a week.

Still, Joey was determined to make it on his own, to prove that he could thrive outside of The Rat Pack without any help from Sinatra.

"Frank and the others have said they would appear [on the show], and I appreciate it," Joey said. "But that's all I have to do now, so people can say I had to go to them for help. If I die, I die by myself. If I make it, I make it by myself."

NBC demanded that some changes be made from the pilot episode that had aired on *The Danny Thomas Show.* Joey would still be playing put-upon schnook Joey Barnes, but he would now be a public-relations man, struggling in the lower echelons of Willoughby Public Relations in New York. The public-relations angle would enable *The Joey Bishop Show* to use celebrity guests if the ratings began to sag. Joey Barnes would be living with his overbearing mother (Madge Blake), but the character of Joey's layabout father, played by Billy Gilbert in the pilot, was jettisoned. "I felt it should be a fatherless home," Joey explained. "Otherwise, why would I be supporting the family, unless my father was lame, retired, or a bum—or why wouldn't I be married or away?"

Joe Flynn, who had played Joey's boss in the pilot, was now re-cast as Joey's brother-in-law. Nancy Hadley would play Joey's secretary/ love interest, and John Griggs—Joey and Sylvia's neighbor back in Englewood—would play Joey's new boss. Marlo Thomas snagged her first regular television role as Joey's kid sister, and newcomer Bill Bixby was added to the cast as Charles Raymond.

Danny Thomas and co-producer Lou Edelman also brought in Broadway actor Warren Berlinger, fresh from Neil Simon's *Come Blow Your Horn,* to play Joey's younger brother, Larry. Marvin Marx, who had written some classic episodes of *The Honeymooners,* was hired as the show's head writer, along with Milt Josefsberg, who had written for Jack Benny for years.

It was obvious to everyone connected with *The Joey Bishop Show* that its star was a nervous wreck as production got under way that summer at Desilu Studios.

"I get there on the first day and walk into the conference room, where there might have been one person who said hello to me," Berlinger said. "I'm sitting there, as an actor normally does, reading through the script and circling my character's name and the words he has to say.

"And Joey walks in. He walks over to me and says, 'I don't want you to do that.' I looked at him and thought that since he was a comic he was being funny, so I laughed and went back to the script and started circling my lines.

"He stopped me by pounding the conference table with his fist. I said, 'Let me understand you, Joey. You don't want me circling my character's name in the script?' And he says, 'Yes—and if I have to tell you again, it's going to be ugly.'"

Berlinger got up, walked out of the room and went back to his hotel, calling his agent at William Morris to tell him he was heading back to New York.

"I started getting calls at the hotel from Danny Thomas, Sheldon Leonard, and a wonderful man named Lou Edelman, who was the executive producer of the show," he said. "So I came in to see Edelman and he charmed the hell out of me. Danny came into the room and said he didn't know what happened, that obviously Joey has a problem with something. So Joey comes into the room and apologizes, saying this is the first time I've done a character on a show, I've always been a stand-up comic, I'm a little uptight about things. He explained that when an actor reads a role the first time around he wants to get the instant and true rhythms of what was written.

"He says it will never happen again, that he looked forward to working with me. He was charming in front of Danny and Sheldon and all his bosses. Well, it only got worse from that point on. Let me put it this way—Marlo and I used to hide in the dressing room from Joey and play Jotto. At one point, on my birthday, Marlo gave me a picture of Joey on a dartboard—and gave me the darts."

NBC, for its part, clearly wanted *The Joey Bishop Show* to succeed. The network gave the show a plum, Wednesday-night timeslot at 8:30 P.M. between ratings winners *Wagon Train* and *The Perry Como Show*. It would compete against *Checkmate* on CBS and a fellow Danny Thomas Productions show, *The Real McCoys*, on ABC.

Mike Dann, who was one of NBC's top programming executives, was instrumental in scheduling *The Joey Bishop Show* that first season.

"To put Joey in between *Wagon Train,* which was a top 10 show, and *Perry Como,* which was also a top 10 show, would be considered a very advantageous position," said Dann. "We at NBC were thrilled because it was a big gamble as to whether or not Joey would make it. He had a good lead-in and lead-out and did just fine that year. It was extraordinary for a guy, in his first year, to hold onto the audience as well as he did that year."

But it was the critics, and not the viewers, who posed problems for *The Joey Bishop Show*, which debuted on September 20, 1961, to almost universal scorn.

"The plot of Wednesday's episode was strictly assembly line, a ho-hum yarn," Harry Harris wrote in *The Philadelphia Inquirer.* "There was little in the proceedings to justify the occasional bursts of laugh-track hilarity.

"Bishop, whose forte is the devastatingly apt ad-lib, contributed little more than pained looks, like a bush-league Jack Benny," Harrison wrote "The considerable charm of which he's capable was manifested only in a P.S. cigaret [*sic*] commercial. Next week's episode will feature Jack and Randy Paar and one of the Marquis chimps. They might help, but less imitative writers would help even more."

"The jokes follow a ritual pattern. A pattern that could, in subsequent weeks . . . become a rut," wrote Harriet Van Horne. However, Van Horne also noted that "Joey Bishop is wonderful. His writers ought to be more appreciative of this treasure."

New York Times television critic Jack Gould was also less than kind. "Mr. Bishop is cast as an aide in a press-agent firm, a figure of Milquetoastian overtones who constantly gets into trouble and is buffeted about by people with louder voices," Gould wrote. "Conceivably the characterization could work out in time, but the premiere left doubts that it will be brought to the surface in a meaningful way. The press agent's adventures . . . completely miss the humor of Mr. Bishop, which lies in his unexpected turn of phrase and mind. Instead, there was substituted only the canned and predictable artificiality that is the recurrent blight of so much filmed TV comedies."

Joey was stung by the criticism. "Those first ten shows—if I could only buy them back, or at least insist that they never be rerun," he said. "We didn't get a good review in the whole country that I can remember. Not that I had to be told. I was the first to say the show was awful. My first reaction was, 'Let me out of this.'"

By November, *The Joey Bishop Show* had settled into a comfortable ratings niche on NBC. Behind-the-scenes, however, it was total chaos as Joey clashed with his writers, producers, directors, and co-stars.

"It was his total distrust of everything that was going on. He just didn't trust anybody," said Berlinger. "I can tell you that Marlo was thrown off the set by Joey because she couldn't handle an imitation of Bette Davis doing 'Peetah, Peetah, Peetah.' She did it rather poorly and Joey went into a rage. We were afraid to say hello to him because he would snap at us. I almost quit the business as a result of that show."

Joey also clashed with Joe Flynn, who was subsequently fired from the show in October. "Joey was like a man in shell-shock," said Flynn. "He was the press's darling and he'd never been attacked before. He began taking the script home at night to 'fix it.' I remember once he was supposed to tell Madge Blake to 'Shut up!' He changed it to, 'Mom, please!' That's how desperately he wanted to be loved. Then when he began to explain to me what a joke was, I knew we were in trouble."

The Hollywood gossip mill whispered that Joey axed Flynn because his co-star was getting too many laughs. The theory was "hokum," Joey said.

"As the star of the show I passed on the material Joe got," he said. "What we felt was, we were running with two sad sacks instead of one, me. In my role as sort of a fall guy I couldn't be pushed around by a character which was written and conceived as lacking in any push whatsoever. Joe was dropped because the chemistry wasn't there between our two respective characters."

Flynn's ouster from *The Joey Bishop Show* was a blessing in disguise for the actor. Shortly thereafter he was cast alongside Ernest Borgnine on *McHale's Navy*, which ran on CBS for six seasons.

The troubles on *The Joey Bishop Show* continued. Shortly after Flynn was fired, Griggs and Hadley were shown the door.

"We were getting the cold-shoulder from Joey and one day he's knocking on everyone's dressing room, saying 'Come with me,'" Berlinger said. "We're now going to *The Dick Van Dyke Show*, which was shooting right across from us. They're rehearsing and we're sitting in the stands, watching them. They're having a ball, having a famous time, laughing at each other, at the material. When they were through Joey turns to us and says, 'Why can't we be like that?!'" Other cast members called the trips from *The Joey Bishop Show* set to *The Dick Van Dyke Show* set "like going from Forest Lawn to Disneyland." The situation was exceedingly tense.

"We did many things wrong," Joey said of that first season. "We violated a very basic concept in comedy. When you have a clever comedian—and in modesty I think I am—you surround him with funny people . . . I made the mistake of working with clever people.

"But the greatest mistake we made was not playing before an audience," he said. "We shot the show like a movie and put in the laughs later. I knew something was wrong when I opened a door and got a big laugh. Then I closed the door and got applause."

In the ratings department, at least, *The Joey Bishop Show* beat *The Dick Van Dyke Show* for the 1961–62 season. *The Joey Bishop Show* ended its first season ranked twenty-fifth among all prime-time shows. That was good enough for NBC to renew the show for a second season. NBC, however, chose to ignore the fact that Joey's lead-in, *Wagon Train*, was the season's top-rated show. The fact that the network went from first at 8 P.M. to twenty-fifth at 8:30 wasn't a good omen.

"It was a mistake to make me a publicity man," Joey said after the smoke had cleared and the show wrapped production on its first season. "What do I know about that? Another thing. You're supposed to start off a series with nine scripts ahead. When I arrived here there wasn't even one finished. Everything was done frantically on the spur of the moment, week to week.

"I knew it wasn't coming off, and I was fighting for my life. I had to do what I could, make the changes I felt were needed."

By today's sitcom standards, it's virtually impossible to judge how good or bad the quality of that first season really was. To this day, Joey refuses to let the first season of *The Joey Bishop Show* be shown on television. When Nickelodeon's TV Land cable network aired *The Joey Bishop Show* for a short time in 1998, it did so only with Joey's stipulation that season one was off-limits. Thirty years and a lifetime later hadn't soothed Joey's feelings about that first season.

Trouble on the Set

aving been burned during that first season, Joey was determined to completely revamp *The Joey Bishop Show* for its second season. NBC would now air the show in color, but it had
moved *The Joey Bishop Show* to a more difficult timeslot, Saturday
nights at 8:30 P.M. *The Joey Bishop Show* would now be sandwiched
between the detective series *Sam Benedict* and the NBC Saturday-
night movie, without the benefit of a healthy *Wagon Train* lead-in.
It was up against the first half-hour of *The Defenders* on CBS and an
ABC sitcom, *Mr. Smith Goes to Washington*. NBC, meanwhile, had
vetoed Joey's request to change the show's name to *The New Joey
Bishop Show* but had agreed to several other revisions.

For starters, Joey Barnes would no longer be a put-upon public-relations schmuck. The character of Joey Barnes was transformed
into a confident talk-show personality, hosting his own self-titled
television show in New York. Not only was this closer to Joey's real-
life persona, but it would give Joey Barnes (and Bishop) the chance
to mix with A-list celebrities who would come to visit his show. Jack
Benny was already lined up for an appearance.

The large cast from the first season was also winnowed down.
Gone from the show were Joey's mother and brother, Warren
Berlinger having already fled back to Broadway to appear in *How
to Succeed in Business without Really Trying*. Joey Barnes would
now be married, with a wisecracking agent/sidekick and a good-
natured handyman who would flit in and out of Joey's plush
Manhattan apartment.

For the role of wife Ellie Barnes, Joey hired curvaceous Abby Dalton, who had co-starred with Jackie Cooper for three seasons in the CBS naval sitcom *Hennesey*. Replacing Berlinger would be Philadelphia comic Guy Marks as Joey's agent, Freddie (named after Joey's brother). Ex-Three Stooges member Joe Besser, also from Philadelphia, would play fey handyman Jillson, while veteran actress Mary Treen was hired to play Hilda, the Barnes' live-in maid (complete with white maid's uniform). Treen appeared on a handful of episodes before being made a regular on the show.

Joey's hiring of Joe Besser came at an opportune time for the roly-poly comedian, who was finding work hard to come by after leaving the Three Stooges (he had replaced Shemp Howard). Besser had been around for years and had gotten his start in vaudeville, graduating to supporting movie roles and a one-season stint on *The Abbott and Costello Show* as Stinky, the spoiled man-child who dressed in a Little Lord Fauntleroy suit and frequently tangled with Lou Costello. In between he had worked with all the big-name comics of the day including Jackie Gleason and Milton Berle, on whose radio show Besser had been a regular.

Besser had first met Joey when he dropped by the set of *Sergeants Three* in Kanab and was surprised to learn that Joey had been a fan of his work for years, dating back to Joey's Army days in San Antonio. "I feel like I've known Joey Besser for years," Joey told Besser and Sammy Davis Jr., who had made the introductions. "When I was in the Army and I was the head of the entertainment division, we owned a print of *Hey Rookie!* We ran that thing for all the servicemen until the sprockets fell off! Finally I had to order a new print!"

Joey promised Besser the two would work together, and sure enough, Besser received a call during the first season of *The Joey Bishop Show*. Joey wanted him to appear as a mailman in an episode called "A Very Warm Christmas." That episode aired in February 1962, and before long Besser had made six appearances on *The Joey Bishop Show*.

After my appearances in the Bishop show aired, NBC received thousands of letters from fans who wrote in and said, "Thank you for finding Joe Besser. We missed him! Besser wrote in his autobiography, *Not Just a Stooge*.

Joey heard about the deluge of mail my appearances on his show had created, so after we filmed the last show of the season, James V. Kern, the show's director, came to me and said, "Joe, we're going to do a new series for next season. It's already been set and I've got news for you. You're going to be a regular, right from the go."

Besser would later credit his role as Jillson on *The Joey Bishop Show* with helping him to "break the curse" of being typecast as a Stooge. Joey helped the cause by having Besser on as a guest when he pinch-hit for Johnny Carson on *The Tonight Show* several months before the new season premiered. Besser was so overwhelmed by the welcome he received from the studio audience that he had to fight back tears.

Meanwhile, there were other changes to the show. Garry Marshall and Fred Freeman, who had written for Joey on *The Jack Paar Show* and for Joey's nightclub act, were flown out to California (at Joey's expense) and hired as writers. They had never written a sitcom script. Joey also brought in his old comedy pal Eddie Rio, who was driving a truck at the time, to produce the show. Danny Thomas had grown tired of butting heads with Joey and refused any hands-on participation. Joey also rousted brother Freddie Bishop, who was working as a maitre d' in Miami, to become the show's "dialogue coach." After all these years, Freddie was finally getting a taste of the big time.

Joey also managed to get in one final dig at Joe Flynn when, in the spring of 1962, NBC aired two "preview" episodes of the new-and-improved *Joey Bishop Show* (sans Abby Dalton, who hadn't yet been cast).

"He's been giving out violent interviews. [He's] real unhappy with us," Joey said of Flynn. "Actually he got mad too soon. We wanted him back as my partner, but after that display of temperament we decided to do without him."

Joey also revisited the big question everyone was asking around town: Why hadn't Frank, Dean, Peter, or Sammy visited *The Joey Bishop Show* that first season to help give it a much-needed boost?

"They all indicated interest. I had one show Frank could have done in about three hours, but he was leaving the next day for Europe," Joey said. "And there was one in which Peter could have played a bachelor who lends me his apartment, but he had to leave the Sunday before we could start shooting.

Jillson (Joe Besser), Joey Barnes, and wife Ellie (Abby Dalton) on the "Penguins Three" episode of The Joey Bishop Show—*the first episode written by Garry Marshall and Fred Freeman.*

"One show had a reference to Frank in a phone conversation, but we needed time, so we cut out the whole scene. My brother-in-law was supposed to sing a song to Sinatra over the phone, but I objected. I felt that mentioning Sinatra without using his voice or offering at least a glimpse of him would be cheating the audience."

The revamped *Joey Bishop Show* premiered in September 1962 to a resounding yawn, both from its audience and the critics. The show's opening graphics were new, with Joey now sitting on a stool and pointing to an animated "book" which, when it opened, featured the show's co-stars. Honorary Rat Packers Sammy Cahn and Jimmy Van Heusen provided Joey with a hummable theme song, which was punctuated by the opening trilling of "Joey, Joey, Joey."

"Joey stood alone on Saturday night and that 8:30 P.M. position was not so good now because NBC had moved their comedies to Wednesday night," said programming exec Mike Dann, who had moved to CBS. "Joey was a victim of scheduling. It is more important in television where you're scheduled than the contents of your show. If it's a fairly good comedy but not a top comedy, and you isolate it or don't give it a good lead-in, the show can't make it. We now know that *The Joey Bishop Show* should have been scheduled later in the evening, at 9:30 or 10 P.M.

"It was the only comedy between two dramas, so Joey had nothing going for him," Dann said. "More than practically any other TV comedy star during the 'Golden Days,' Joey was the victim of scheduling."

The revamped *Joey Bishop Show* wasn't a bad sitcom. It could, in fact, be quite charming at times. The plots were simple and gentle, reflecting Joey's "attitude" of not roiling the waters or offending anyone. On the surface, there seemed to be a good chemistry between Joey and Guy Marks. Joe Besser's handyman, Jillson—a distant TV cousin of Art Carney's Ed Norton—provided some comic relief and soon became a fan favorite (Besser was even made an honorary member of the local janitor's union). Abby Dalton had a tendency to overact, but she played the role of the early 1960s housewife well. Dalton's Ellie Barnes, however, didn't have the edge (temperamental and/or sexual) of Mary Tyler Moore's Laura Petrie over on *The Dick Van Dyke Show*, where they were having all that fun.

The Joey Bishop Show plots, such as they were, usually found Joey Barnes in a bind. How can he stop Freddie from crashing his three-month wedding anniversary dinner with Ellie? How can Joey cure Ellie of her shopping addiction (and stop her from letting in those door-to-door salesmen)? Should Joey take a much-needed vacation and let an unknown comic (played by Corbett Monica) take his place on the show—and perhaps do better than Joey? Joey

Domestic bliss in the Barnes household.

is about to perform for the governor, but he can't find his cufflinks. And so on.

Garry Marshall and Fred Freeman found that working for Joey on a regular basis wasn't exactly a bed of roses. Joey was tough on all of his writers and could be verbally abusive, even to the new guys. Joey seemed to take an immediate dislike to Freeman, a college graduate and burgeoning playwright who considered TV writing beneath him, something to fill the time until he wrote the Great American Play.

"At the time I was young and pretentious and Joey would get pissed off at me, calling me 'College Boy, College Boy,'" Freeman said. "Garry was much better with comics than I was, because he was kind of a comic himself. It rolled off his back. There was a lot of tension between me and Joey, and probably if I was a little more mature I would have understood it better. I made the mistake of disagreeing with Joey—a lot."

Freeman's attitude eventually cost him his job. One day, in a closed-door script meeting with Joey, Freeman complained that "the protagonist wouldn't do that"—his use of the word "protagonist" immediately raising Joey's hackles.

"I think Joey was an inherently bright guy but because he hadn't been to college he had a complex about it," Freeman said. "When I used the word 'protagonist,' Joey grabbed me by the collar and lifted me off the ground and almost hit me. He said, 'If you don't like it, you can get out of here,' and I said, 'OK, I will,' and that's when he grabbed me. Garry and I split up on that show. I said, 'Garry, you can stay if you want to' and he was pragmatic so he said, 'OK.'"

It wasn't any easier for Marvin Marx, a holdover from the first season who was a mentor figure for Marshall and Freeman.

"Marvin Marx was a kind of professional whipping boy who worked for Jackie Gleason, Betty Hutton, and then for Joey," Freeman said. "There was one time when Marvin was working on a very difficult script and had to rewrite it. Joey was making Marvin crazy.

"Finally it got to the point where Joey said OK, he was satisfied. It was about 6 or 7 in the evening and we had a birthday cake for

Marvin. We were in his office when Joey comes in out of nowhere, throws the script on the table and says, 'This is shit!' or words to that effect. It was the first time I had seen a grown man cry. Marvin just lost it. He quit a few weeks later and took me on as his partner on Jackie Gleason's *American Scene Magazine*."

Joey's anger also found a target in co-star Guy Marks, the fellow South Philadelphia comedian who was hired to play Freddie, Joey Barnes' agent. Joey fired Marks in January, soon after the show's nineteenth episode, "Freddie Goes Highbrow," in which Freddie fakes a British accent to impress his society girlfriend.

Marks felt ambushed by his firing and lashed back at Joey in the press. He said he was "surprised and shocked" at his dismissal and pointed to the "Freddie Goes Highbrow" episode as hastening his departure.

"It's all about me," he said of the episode. "I took over the whole show for the one night, and some people think it hurt Bishop to sit back and watch me romp.

"We can't figure out what bothered him," Marks said of Joey. "Maybe I was coming off too strong. Some people seemed to think so. They warned me, 'Watch yourself, if you get any better you'll have to go.' The way Joe Flynn did last year.

"The last meeting I had with Joey in his office he had a fit of temper, and I couldn't talk to him," Marks said. "He obviously wanted me off the show . . . He put an ad in *Variety* saying that I was terribly talented, but I couldn't play second banana, that I had left the studio 10 days ago and he hadn't heard from me since.

"I asked for a retraction, and then I put my own ad in *Variety*. I said I did NOT leave the show, that I appreciated what it had done for my career and that I regretted that what Bishop called 'a conflict of personalities offstage' had resulted in an unexpected vacation.

"I didn't take the initiative," Marks said. "It came as a shock. It was tough to be treated that way by a guy from Philadelphia."

With Marks out of the picture, *Joey Bishop Show* writers Milt Josefsberg, Harry Crane, and others were forced to write around the character of Freddie for the remainder of the season, which wrapped in April 1963. The show's future was still uncertain. *The Joey Bishop Show* had failed to crack the top 25 that season, and there would

Joey tries to convince Ellie that his mustache makes him look more debonair.

have to be even more revamping if NBC decided to bring the show back for a third go-round. Marks would have to be replaced, and several new writers would have to be hired (Garry Marshall had followed Fred Freeman out the door).

"I always thought of Joey as a perfectionist," Besser wrote in his memoirs. "If one line of dialogue was off he would work on it until he got it right, many times right up until minutes before we filmed.

"One time, I vividly recall the day Joey tried changing a line of dialogue on me before I made my entrance—but it backfired on him. Joey frequently did this to others in the show, but this time he didn't give me fair warning. Joey and I were supposed to make our entrance together through the apartment door. We were standing behind the door when Joey stopped me. His exact words to me were: 'Joey, when you come in don't say this line say that.' When our director, James V. Kern, rolled the cameras, I walked in and repeated exactly what Joey told me to say . . . Well, Joey busted up laughing and, in the future, he never changed a line on me at the spur of the moment like that again."

In the meantime, Joey was preparing for the next Rat Pack movie, *Robin and the Seven Hoods*, a gangster comedy Sinatra was planning to begin filming that fall. Dean and Sammy were in, but Peter was out of the movie, The Rat Pack, and Sinatra's life altogether. President Kennedy and his brother, Attorney General Robert Kennedy, had dispatched the Brother-in-Lawford to Sinatra's Palm Springs hideaway to inform Frank that the president wouldn't be staying there as planned. Sinatra had spent a fortune renovating the estate in anticipation of Kennedy's arrival, building a new wing of suites and installing a helicopter pad. But Sinatra's alleged mob ties wouldn't be good for President Kennedy's image, and it was decided (to add insult to injury) that Kennedy would hunker down with Bing Crosby—Sinatra's arch rival. When Lawford broke the news to Sinatra, Frank went ballistic, hurling Peter down a flight of stairs and vowing never to speak to him again. He never did, save for a short phone call he made to Lawford after Frank Jr. was kidnapped (asking the Brother-in-Lawford to get Attorney General Robert Kennedy involved in the investigation).

Joey, however, was still in Sinatra's good graces. Curiously, though, two troubled seasons of *The Joey Bishop Show* had gone by without a cameo appearance by The Leader (or Dean, Sammy, or Peter, for that matter). Joey signed a $75,000 contract for his role in *Robin and the Seven Hoods*, which was to be directed by Gene Kelly.

And then, just like that, Joey was out of the movie. Rat Pack watchers, who studied the group like historians scrutinized Kruschev's Kremlin, pointed to Joey's prima donna behavior as the reason for his banishment from *Robin and the Seven Hoods*. The story went that Sinatra had asked Joey, at the last minute, to fill in for a weekend at The Cal-Neva Lodge in Lake Tahoe (Frank and Dean owned a piece of the action).

Several people familiar with the story all told the same version: "Joey started making all these demands, like having Sinatra's plane take him to Lake Tahoe. And he wanted to bring an entourage and wanted more money. Frank was stunned at first, then said, 'Fuck him. Give him what he wants, but remember from now on, fuck him.' And that was the end of Joey with Frank."

If Joey was disappointed, he didn't show it, at least not publicly. In all the interviews he granted around that time, he never once mentioned *Robin and the Seven Hoods* or alluded to any problems with Sinatra. He did spend a good amount of newsprint talking about his permanent move to Hollywood. He and Sylvia had finally sold the house in Englewood and had bought a stately three-bedroom mansion in Beverly Hills, complete with a guest house, maid's room, and pool. Ernest Borgnine and movie mogul Jack Warner lived next door. Joey and Sylvia enjoyed throwing Sunday-night bagels-and-lox parties for pals like Milton Berle, Herkie Styles, and Jack Benny. The goodies were supplied by Max Asnas, who owned the Stage Deli in Manhattan. Asnas would actually fly out to Los Angeles with the chopped liver, whitefish, etc., for Joey and his pals.

Larry, now 16, enrolled in Beverly Hills High, where he became close friends with Rob Reiner, Richard Dreyfuss, and Albert Einstein (who would later change his name to Albert Brooks).

While *The Joey Bishop Show* hadn't exactly set the world on fire during its first two seasons, NBC decided to bring it back for season number three. But the network's patience was beginning to wear thin. Joey had, for the most part, failed to deliver the goods, though his name was still big enough to draw a modest viewing audience. He was still packing 'em in at The Sands, and although his relationship with Sinatra was, for the moment, imperiled, the Rat Pack aura still held a certain cachet for NBC programmers. There was already talk among the network brass of giving Joey his own variety show if *The Joey Bishop Show* failed in its third incarnation. The new season would include several more changes, including the casting of Joey's

Joey returned to The Sands in 1963, where he welcomed the world champion Los Angeles Dodgers and stars Moose Skowron, Ron Perranoski, Don Drysdale, Tommy Davis, Frank Howard, and Willie Davis (left to right). That's Joey's agent, Norman Brokaw (second from left) with his sons Sandy, Joel, and David. (Courtesy Sandy Brokaw)

Beverly Hills neighbor, Corbett Monica, to play the role of Larry, Joey's manager/sidekick. Like Guy Marks before him, Monica would play a bachelor, giving the show's writers opportunities to feature subplots revolving around Larry's love life.

It was also decided that Joey and Ellie, married for one TV season, would become parents in their second year of wedded sitcom bliss. Abby Dalton had just given birth to a son, Matthew David Smith, who was recruited to play the Barnes' newborn son, Joey Jr.

Joey also spoke hopefully of the upcoming season, having recruited Andy Williams, Bob Hope, Edgar Bergen, and Phil Foster, among others, as guest stars.

It didn't make a difference. The new-and-improved *Joey Bishop Show* followed the same ratings path as the first two seasons, averaging lackadaisical ratings numbers and finishing nowhere near the top twenty-five. The new writers who had joined the show, including Carl Kleinschmitt and Dale McRaven, seemed to bear the brunt of Joey's anger.

"One of Joey's lines when he didn't like the script was, 'Fellas, I know you've been working fourteen to sixteen hours a day, but you haven't been doing your homework,'" said McRaven. "He didn't like writers, didn't like to admit someone did stuff that he didn't, so we were always treated like garbage. But he treated everyone like garbage.

"In the year-and-a-half Carl and I were with the show, Joey never once called us by our names—we were always 'The Fellas,'" McRaven said. "Even if it was me alone he'd say, 'Hi, fellas.' The only time he ever mentioned us by name was when he hurt his back and was in the hospital. Garry [Marshall] went to see him and he said to Garry, 'Where are those assholes Kleinschmitt and McRaven?' We were scum because we'd deserted him."

Sam Denoff wrote a few *Joey Bishop Show* episodes with his partner, Bill Persky, before they left and created *That Girl* with ex-*Bishop Show* co-star Marlo Thomas.

"I'll tell you the ultimate actor's story," said Denoff. "Someone had written a script for the show in which Joey Barnes' long-lost brother shows up. It was very wonderfully written and was very funny. The producer, Milt Josefsberg, one of the classic great comedy writers, loved the script.

"So now they rehearse it and it's one of those shows that are good. The crew and everybody were laughing because Joey was so good playing two parts.

"On the morning of the day they're supposed to shoot the episode, Joey shows up in Milt's office. He says, 'Milt, I'm not gonna do the show, it's not gonna work, it's wrong. I'm angry at you for not realizing it's not funny.'

"So Milt says, 'What's wrong with it?' And Joey says, 'I'll tell you what's wrong with it—my brother is getting all the laughs!'"

By February 1964, with the show's ratings continuing to falter, word leaked out that Joey had met with NBC about the possibility of hosting a variety show. *The Joey Bishop Show* looked like a goner.

"First I read in the papers that my show would be canceled. Then I was told by NBC not to believe it," Joey said. "They said that until you've been notified you're canceled, don't believe it. Well, I haven't been notified, but I don't know where I stand, either. I'm not going to make the mistake of being rushed into a variety show just three weeks after we end the season on the comedy."

Joey made it clear to NBC that, if they wanted him to host the variety show, they would have to give him a year to assemble a cast and crew. But NBC didn't want to wait that long.

With Joey balking at the variety show offer and *The Joey Bishop Show* continuing to be a ratings drain, NBC decided to cut its losses and cancelled the show in late spring of 1964. CBS, needing something—anything—to throw onto its faltering Sunday-night schedule, snapped up *The Joey Bishop Show* for the 1964–65 season. Joey would now be on the CBS schedule between *My Living Doll* at 9 and *Candid Camera* at 10 P.M. He had finally gotten the later timeslot everyone seemed to think his show deserved.

"Sunday was our weakest night," said CBS programming executive Mike Dann. "By that time, *The Ed Sullivan Show* was declining and we didn't know what to do with Sunday night. It was terrible. Putting *The Joey Bishop Show* there shows how weak we were. We were experimenting with anything." The final NBC episode of *The Joey Bishop Show* had ended, ironically enough, with Joey, Ellie, and Joey Jr. moving into an NBC penthouse. Joey decided to use the awkward situation as comic fodder for the opening show on CBS—the network for which Joey Barnes now worked after his NBC talk show was cancelled.

"We are even writing in some of the actual dialogue I had with both NBC and CBS," Joey said. "When they first telephoned me about moving to CBS, I said, 'If they want to put the show on after 2 A.M., forget it.'"

CBS, figuring it had nothing to lose, decided to tinker with the show, which now went through its fourth evolution. Rusty Hamer, who had starred on *Make Room for Daddy*, was brought on board as Ellie's younger, college-aged brother. A girlfriend was found for

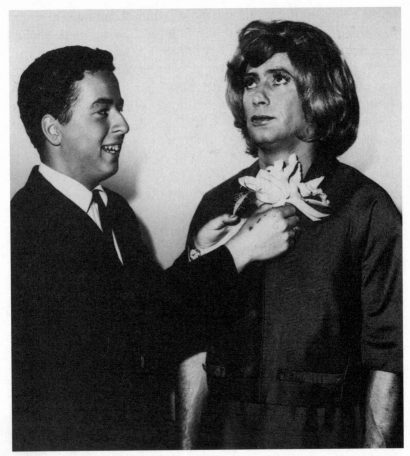

Rusty (Rusty Hamer) adjusts Uncle Joey's corsage after Joey agrees to dress in drag for Rusty's fraternity.

Larry (Corbett Monica remained with the show). And *The Joey Bishop Show* was now airing in black-and-white again for the first time since its first season.

"RCA had won the color battle and underwrote color programming by paying below-the-line production costs on shows like *All Star Revue, Colgate Comedy Hour,* and *Show of Shows,*" Dann said. "After about eleven or twelve years of some color, Nielsen started to show that color was a distinct advantage, that you had a

7 to 9 percent advantage if you were in color. Everyone in black-and-white was at a disadvantage . . . and Joey was a victim of that."

Joey was also, once again, a victim of scheduling. *The Joey Bishop Show*, after moving to CBS, had the misfortune of going up against the last half-hour of *Bonanza* on NBC.

Although things weren't looking very bright on the series front, Joey continued to perform regularly in Vegas, where he was now joined on stage by old pal Mel Bishop. Mel, like Rummy, worked as a solo act after leaving the Bishop Brothers and had appeared in episodic television shows and few small movie roles (including *Sergeants 3*). Joey had hired Mel as a sort of aide-de-camp the previous year, giving him small roles on *The Joey Bishop Show*, among other more mundane duties.

"He had a young fellow working for him and one day I got a call from Joey's manager, Ed Hookstratten, asking if I wanted to work for Joey," Mel said. "Ed said, 'Joey needs someone he can lean on, someone he can bullshit with, someone he can yell at.' He told me what the salary was and it was more than I was making—and it was a steady job."

And so it was that half of the old Bishop Brothers comedy act was reborn at The Sands. Joey dragged out his mandolin, played "In a Little Spanish Town," and kibitzed with the audience. Soon thereafter, Mel, dressed in a waiter's uniform, came onstage carrying a piece of paper.

"I have the note in one hand and Joey's trying to play his mandolin faster and faster and I'm oblivious," said Mel. "Finally I walk over to him and he looks at me and I say, 'Do you know "Sweethearts?" He doesn't know it—and now he knows he's lost the audience—so finally I give him the note, telling him it's from 'the boss,' who of course was [Sands chief] Jack Entratter.

"And the note says, 'Take that mandolin and shove it up your ass.' It was very, very funny. Then Joey would call me back onstage and I would sing a legitimate song."

Joey, the ever-present sub, was also called upon to pinch-hit for other acts at The Sands, including Nat King Cole and Jerry Lewis. Lewis had injured his eye in an explosion on his boat and had to bow out of a Sands appearance. Jack Entratter called Joey, who flew to Vegas at the last minute.

"Joey and I went on stage, and when we came off, Joey got a standing ovation," said Mel Bishop. "But then we started hearing more laughs. Jerry Lewis had gone back out again, so Joey says to Jack Entratter, 'Jack, we got the next plane home. I came up here to do the guy a favor, and I'm doing him a favor, and if he can't take the fact that I'm doing him a favor and he's gotta get his laughs, I'm going home.'" Joey always seemed to harbor a special dislike for Lewis. Years later, when he was living in Newport Beach, Joey was

Hosting the Emmy Awards (1964).

Guest star Buddy Hackett cuts loose on The Joey Bishop Show.

acting as the goodwill ambassador of sorts for the Newport Beach Yacht Club. He heard that Lewis had docked his boat at the club and went to say hello. As Joey related the story, somewhat disgustedly, he knocked and Lewis opened the door to his cabin, and said to Joey, "Who told you I was here?"

Joey also hosted the Emmy Awards again. This time, the awards were embroiled in controversy. ABC and CBS announced they were boycotting the Emmys just two weeks before the ceremonies were scheduled to air on NBC. Both networks cited unfairness in the Emmy eligibility process and encouraged their employees to boycott the show, which was being hosted by Johnny Carson in New York and Joey out in Hollywood.

"I guess we're going through with it," Joey quipped at the beginning of the telecast. "The entire Emmy affair may consist of just me and Price-Waterhouse. I bid you welcome to one of the greatest fights of the century. The NBC peacock got its feather in CBS's eye. Should NBC decide to pull out tonight, there'll be immediate dancing. Win or lose, the secret word is jealousy!"

That same month, the Friar's Club roasted Joey for the second time, this time at the Waldorf-Astoria in New York City, where Joey was feted as "Entertainer of the Year." Jack E. Leonard emceed the event, with the star-studded guest list including Jan Murray, *Joey Bishop Show* co-star Corbett Monica, Buddy Hackett, Danny Thomas, Sidney Poitier, Steve Lawrence, The McGuire Sisters, and Sammy Davis Jr.

Joey received a congratulatory telegram from President Lyndon Johnson, but telegrams from Jack Ruby ("May the Dallas police watch over you!") and Frank Sinatra ("Come to Hawaii and I'll give you a swimming lesson!") were deemed fishy at best. Leonard predicted that CBS chief James Aubrey would lose his job over his decision to acquire *The Joey Bishop Show*, while Jan Murray quipped, "I could talk about Joey and his wonderful accomplishments . . . for another minute or so, easy."

Joey might have been quick with a zinger, but CBS wasn't laughing when it premiered *The Joey Bishop Show* in September 1964 to the same old results. The show's move to CBS, and the subsequent retooling, didn't help in the ratings department. Nor did it

Arguing over a golf club in the CBS premiere of The Joey Bishop Show, *1964.*

help that the show was now airing in black-and-white again—just as color was gaining prominence across the television landscape.

There wasn't a whole lot Joey could do to drum up interest in his show. It didn't matter that guest stars like Oscar Levant visited *The Joey Bishop Show* that season or that Abby Dalton discovered that she was pregnant again. CBS and the show's writers hoped that Dalton's pregnancy, which was written into the show's storyline, would stir some interest as Joey and Ellie Barnes awaited the birth

Guest stars like Oscar Levant couldn't help save The Joey Bishop Show *once it moved from NBC to CBS—which cancelled the show after one season. (Courtesy CBS Photo Archive)*

of their second child. But it didn't seem to matter, and CBS cancelled the show in the spring of 1965. That left Joey without a steady job for the first time in nearly five years. The NBC variety-show offer was now off the table, and the Rat Pack movies had fizzled out. *Robin and the Seven Hoods* (minus Peter and Joey) was released in 1964 to a collective yawn. The Rat Pack era had, for all intents and purposes, ended with President Kennedy's assassination on November 22, 1963.

Joey's contact with Sinatra since being thrown off *Robin and the Seven Hoods* had been minimal. Frank never did make it onto *The Joey Bishop Show*, but Joey had finally gotten back into Sinatra's good graces the year before. Sinatra was swimming in Hawaii with a woman friend when they were pulled out to sea by the strong undertow. He probably would have drowned if not for broad-shouldered actor Brad Dexter, who dove into the surf and dragged Frank and his friend back to safety. Joey sent Frank a telegram: "I thought you could walk on water." Sinatra loved it and invited Joey to join him, Dean, and Sammy for a 1965 charity show benefiting Dismas House in St. Louis. It would be a sort of mini Rat Pack reunion that would be shown via closed-circuit television in movie theaters in New York and Los Angeles. But Joey had thrown his back out and was confined to bed, forcing him to miss the show. Johnny Carson, subbing for Joey, joked that Joey had slipped a disk "backing out of Frank's presence." It was a remark that continued to rankle with Joey thirty-five years later.

Joey had another, fleeting, chance to work with Sinatra that same year, when Frank made a rare appearance on *The Tonight Show* along with Sammy Davis Jr. Joey, subbing for host Johnny Carson, joked about The Leader in his monologue ("He spoke to me backstage. He said, 'Get out of my way'") but didn't have too much time to schmooze, since Sinatra spent only a few minutes chit-chatting before singing one song and leaving the show.

"For me as a comedian, Frank was great. One of the best audiences you could ever have," Joey said. "There was one night when I thought he would never stop laughing. Frank, Dean, and I were doing a charity show, and Prince Philip of England was there as the honored guest.

"The prince comes over, puts his hand on Frank's shoulder and says: 'Aha, the prince and the pauper.' I shoot back to the prince, 'Hell, I didn't know you were broke.' I thought Frank was going to collapse laughing. Then I look at Dean and to the prince and I tell the prince: 'Don't forget to tell Dean tomorrow that he was here today.'

"That night, every time Frank started to sing a song, he'd start to laugh every time he looked at me. That was the way it was for all those years."

*Dean, Joey, and Frank reunited for a mini-Summit at The Sands in April 1966—
one of the last times Joey and Frank worked together. (Courtesy Sands Hotel Collection,
University of Nevada, Las Vegas Library)*

In 1966, Joey joined Frank and Dean (but no Sammy) at a
Summit reunion show at The Sands. They dragged out the rolling
liquor cart and reprised the shtick that had electrified Las Vegas a
scant six years earlier. It had all been fresh and new then; now, it
seemed old and stale, the product of a bygone era. The 1966
Summit reunion would be the last time Joey would ever perform
with Sinatra.

"TV made it impossible for the Rat Pack to survive," Joey said.
"Dean Martin and Sammy Davis had their own shows, and so did I.
We just couldn't drop everything at a moment's notice and get
together like we could when we were all in Vegas, playing clubs.

"Besides, as time goes on, you get into different ways of life.
The Rat Pack was something you graduated from."

Later that year, Sinatra called Joey and asked him to emcee a star-studded fund raiser in Hollywood for California governor Pat Brown. Brown, a Democrat, was running for re-election against former actor Ronald Reagan, a longtime Democrat who had crossed party lines and was now running on the Republican ticket.

Reagan posed a formidable challenge to Brown, who hoped his old pal Sinatra—who had worked so hard to help get John F. Kennedy elected president in 1960—could pull off the same magic six years later, with Joey's help and the comedy of top guests Rowan & Martin. Joey, of course, agreed—and brought the house down.

You got a nice place here. I've been in cities smaller than this. I also want to thank the entertainment committee for the wonderful dressing room accommodations. They gave me a gorgeous room done in white tile. I don't need six sinks, I don't wash that often. On a night like this you can all bow your heads and thank God you're Democrats . . . because if you weren't, instead of the show you're about to see you'd be watching a rerun of Death Valley Days. *You wanna change the lights, I think I'm peeling! We've got a great show, and it's gonna be a real pleasure for me because all I have to do is introduce the acts.*

In a few minutes you're gonna meet two of my drunken friends. God bless Frank. Frank Sinatra taught me how to drink. He had me drunk one night, boy, I was walking around with a snake in my hand trying to kill a stick. And God bless Dean . . . he's backstage lying flat on his face. I says, Dean, let me get you a chair, he says, no, let me stand here like this. And of course the other member of our group, Mr. Sammy Davis Jr. Heaven bless him, I was back East a few months ago when he called me to go to synagogue with him. I felt a little guilty I was responsible for his conversion. He wanted me to turn colored I said go to hell! I got a bad back, I can't march. I'm about to tell you now a true story involving my very dear friend Sammy and myself and you must accept my word that it is true. Sammy did call me to go to synagogue with him. I said okay Sam, what time? He says 9 o'clock. I said I can't make it at 9, I'll meet you there at 9:30 or quarter of 10. He said okay, I'll be sitting in the third row. Like if he don't tell me where he's sitting in synagogue I ain't gonna find him! I said for heaven's sake wear a white skullcap so I'll spot you! Sammy thinks he's Jewish, wait until he tries to walk across water. I'll tell you one thing, boy when he sings "Let my people go" you're gonna see a crowd!

He had some trouble down in Selma, Alabama. He went down for the freedom march, got into a bus. Driver said you'll have to sit to the rear. Sammy says I'm Jewish! The driver says, get off!

May I please now pass onto you my favorite story. Story of a Texan who visits Israel and says to a farmer, I wanna see the biggest ranch in Israel. Farmer shows it to him, 1½ acres. Texan says, you must be kidding, 1½ acres. Back home in Texas I got a ranch, I get in my car 7 o'clock in the morning, ride around in my car until 7 o'clock at night and I still ain't seen all my ranch. Little Jewish fellow says, hey, I once had a car like that!

Ladies and gentleman, here he is, direct from the bar . . . Dean Martin!

10
CHAPTER

The New King of Late Night?

Frank was now out of the picture, but Joey still had one last hurrah with Dean, who was now hosting a popular NBC variety show. Dean was also churning out several movies a year in his singular, sweat-free style and had a particular fondness for Westerns. Joey had always enjoyed Dean's company and jumped at the chance to co-star with him in *Texas Across the River,* a silly comic Western that would tax neither man's acting ability. Joey, bronzed with makeup and wearing the requisite headdress-with-feather, played Kronk, a monosyllabic American Indian and chief of the Kronkaway tribe. Kronk's friend, Sam Hollis (Dean), is a laid-back cowboy enamored of Louisiana debutante Phoebe Ann Naylor (Rosemary Forsyth). Phoebe's marriage to dashing Mexican Don Andrea de Baldasar (Alain Delon) was interrupted by the cavalry. Now, Don Andrea has crossed the river into Texas (hence the movie's title) and met up with Kronk and Hollis to embark on a series of misadventures.

Texas across the River opened to mostly negative reviews in late 1966. *The New York Times* review noted "Accompanying Mr. Martin is Joey Bishop as an Indian named Kronk who is totally without spirit and given to flat remarks, such as 'White man speak with forked tongue. Old Indian saying. All old Indians say it.' Or, when asked why he wasn't born a Comanche, answers, 'Mother ran too fast.'"

Joey took offense to a reporter wondering why a Philadelphia Jew would make a good Indian ("Everybody looks like an Indian once they put on a wig and a headband," he snapped). But, once again, Joey made it clear that television, and not the movies, was where he belonged.

"I don't think there's a place for me in films," he said. "I don't look funny enough for international audiences."

But he was funny enough for American TV audiences. Jack Paar, tiring of his constant battles with NBC, had retired from the daily television grind in 1962, saving himself for the occasional special. Joey was one of many celebrities (Jerry Lewis, Groucho Marx, Art Linkletter, Mort Sahl, and Donald O'Connor) who subbed on the *Tonight Show* until NBC named Johnny Carson as Paar's permanent replacement. Carson, a quick-witted Nebraskan, had made his name as a writer for Red Skelton and as host of the CBS game show *Who Do You Trust?* He took along his *Trust?* sidekick Ed McMahon when he moved to NBC, attempting to fill Paar's large late-night shoes.

By 1966, Carson had not only filled Paar's shoes but had exceeded NBC's wildest expectations, establishing himself and the *Tonight Show* as appointment viewing. The 90-minute show was taped in New York, and Joey, as he had done with Paar, became a frequent *Tonight Show* guest host. And he was needed frequently, since Carson began accruing ridiculous amounts of vacation time after numerous contractual battles with NBC.

The whispers about Joey hosting his own late-night talk show had begun years before when he subbed for Paar. And they had continued when the NBC variety show idea was floated during the ill-fated run of *The Joey Bishop Show.*

Back then, Joey had demanded at least a year to prepare such a show. Now, a year later and with no regular offers coming in, it was looking more and more like a good idea.

CBS and ABC were aware of the reported $25 million Carson was bringing in for NBC and were beginning to make rumblings of their own about launching late-night shows. CBS had its eyes on Merv Griffin, who was hosting his own syndicated talk show for Group W. The United Network, a small syndicator with few stations, had even launched a late-night talk show in Las Vegas, hosted by Bill Dana.

ABC had experimented in late night with Les Crane, but it hadn't worked out. Early in 1966, ABC programming executives

The Jewish Indian: Joey and Dean as Kronk and Sam Hollis in Texas across the River *(1966).*

approached Joey's agent, Norman Brokaw, about the idea of Joey hosting a show for ABC's late-night lineup.

"What happened was, they were doing a benefit for Sam Goldwyn, for his eightieth birthday," Joey said. "All the stars were there, Groucho Marx, Danny Kaye, Milton Berle, Bob Hope. Abe Lastfogel decided to put me on last, and I couldn't believe it. I was sitting there wracking my brain, thinking how am I going to top these guys?

"Now mind you, this is Sam Goldwyn, the head of MGM. My opening line stole the show. I walked over to Goldwyn and said, 'Mr. Goldberg, how are you sir?' The audience froze. Did he make a goof? Then I said, 'The people in the audience don't know how long we know each other, Mr. Goldberg.'

"Tom Moore, the head of ABC, said anybody who's got that kind of guts deserves his own talk show."

It was an alluring proposition but one rife with risks. Not only would Joey be taking on Carson—by now the undisputed, unchallenged king of late-night—but he would be faced with ABC's weak affiliate lineup. Unlike NBC and CBS, ABC was a virtual newcomer to the network TV game with only fifteen years under its belt. ABC had only about 144 affiliate stations covering roughly 75 percent of the U.S. It was considered the weak sister of the three networks, and its affiliates had been content to run movies opposite the *Tonight Show*, which was seen on 210 stations nationwide. There was also no guarantee that ABC affiliates would agree to carry an unproven talk show, since they were staying afloat airing movies.

And if Joey decided to accept ABC's offer, he would have to give up his lucrative nightclub bookings, at least for the foreseeable future, to devote his time and energy to formulating the show.

ABC's idea was to have Joey host a show from Hollywood where, the network reasoned, celebrities might be more likely to appear as guests in their own backyard. Joey's recent reunion with Frank and Dean at The Sands had ABC suits giddy with visions of late-night Rat Pack reunions dancing in their heads (even though none of the Rat Packers had ever showed up on *The Joey Bishop Show*).

There were several upsides for Joey, including the reported $2 million ABC would pay him for the weeknight show. It worked out to $569,000, guaranteed, for thirty-nine weeks. There was also the fact that the proposed studio was situated on Hollywood and Vine, only minutes from Joey's Beverly Hills home. Joey certainly didn't need the money; wise real estate investments had paid off handsomely, and his sold-out appearances in Vegas, Tahoe, and Miami Beach had transformed the poor South Philadelphia kid into a bona fide millionaire. The financial windfall from his half-ownership in *The Joey Bishop Show* never came to pass, since the show didn't hit in syndication, but Joey was financially secure. He drove a Rolls-Royce Silver Cloud around Beverly Hills, swam laps in his backyard pool, and had moved his parents out of South Philly and into a place in Miami Beach.

Joey's comfortable lifestyle had even enabled him to get a $5,000 hair transplant to offset his famous black buzzcut, receding now as he neared fifty. If he and Frank didn't share The Rat Pack anymore, they did share Dr. Sammy Ayres, who performed Joey's transplant before moving on to Sinatra's thinning scalp.

Joey and Sylvia had been in New York with Sinatra and his new girlfriend, Mia Farrow. The press had been buzzing about rumors that Sinatra was about to marry Farrow. Sinatra had offered Joey a tux for an appearance on *What's My Line?* but had to think for a moment if he could spare it. Joey guessed (correctly) that Sinatra wouldn't need the tux because he would be wearing a suit while getting married to Farrow. Joey broke the news of the Sinatra–Farrow nuptials to a stunned *Tonight Show* audience while subbing for Carson.

By July 1966 the talk-show deal with ABC had leaked into the press. Ironically, it was just as Joey was set to guest-host for Carson on the *Tonight Show*. "I know I'd rather do something I fit into than something I don't fit into," Joey told columnist Earl Wilson. "I don't want to do any more series. That one I did never won any prizes." Always thinking ahead, Joey had already worked out a handshake deal with NBC vice-president Dave Tebet. If the ABC show failed, Tebet had agreed to take Joey back for seven weeks a year as Carson's sub. "We're very good friends, and if Joey goes with ABC, I can only wish him luck and say I'm sorry we don't have him," Tebet said diplomatically.

Joey had already met with ABC affiliates via closed-circuit television to help sell his new talk show. Seated at the apron of a Hollywood sound stage, he sounded confident that he could be the one to topple Carson.

"The [Carson] show is taken for granted. There is no excitement in it and no sense of something new happening," he told the affiliates. "We are planning as well as you plan a Broadway play. We have analyzed it to the *n*th degree. I think it's going to be a big hit. I am grateful for your faith in me." Joey might have been grateful,

but the affiliates weren't so sure. A third of them opted to keep running their late-night movies instead of airing Joey's show. The risk
was just too high.

In August, ABC officially announced the deal: *The Joey Bishop
Show* would begin airing in April 1967, with a minimum commit-
ment of twenty-six weeks. That could be stretched to thirty-nine
weeks depending on the show's success. The ninety-minute show
would air live on the East Coast and would be tape-delayed on the
West Coast at a Hollywood studio yet to be determined. "I fought
for it," Joey said of airing the show live. "The others are all on tape,
and I feel this kind of show should be live. Also, there's a different
kind of studio audience if you do the show in Hollywood at 6:30 or
9:30. One's daytime; the other, theater."

Paul Orr, who had produced *The Jack Paar Show*, would produce *The Joey Bishop Show*. Where Carson had Skitch Henderson as
his musical conductor, Joey would have Johnny Mann and His
Merry Men. As for Joey's sidekick, no one had yet been chosen.
ABC was hurriedly conducting a nationwide search.

"The only thing I'm planning to do is get paid," Joey said of his
new undertaking. "Seriously, we're leaving it as vague as possible.
We hope it will come up as pure honesty, one of those things where
we'll tell the people, 'Don't write letters today because we're changing it tomorrow.'"

"Ours will be more or less a probing type of thing," he said of
his new show. "We'll have people from show business, politics,
sports, writing—anybody with something important or interesting
to say, and we'll try to uncover things about our guests that aren't
generally known."

With the talk show still months away, Joey began work on a new
movie, *Who's Minding the Mint?*, in which he played Italian plumber
Ralph Randazzo. Ralph is part of a gang recruited by hapless U.S. mint
worker Harry Lucas (Jim Hutton), who accidentally lost $50,000 at
the mint and schemes to break into the place and replace the cash. The
cast was a good one; besides Joey and Hutton, it boasted Milton Berle,
Dorothy Provine, Bob Denver, Victor Buono, Jack Gilford, and Jamie
Farr. *Your Show of Shows* alum Howard Morris directed the picture,
which opened to good reviews and brisk box-office business.

The cast of Who's Minding the Mint? *(from left): Victor Buono, Jack Gilford, Joey, Walter Brennan, Dorothy Provine, Jim Hutton, Bob Denver, and Milton Berle (on the staircase). (The Kobal Collection)*

Around the same time, Gene Kelly approached Joey about making a cameo appearance in *A Guide for the Married Man*, a movie Kelly was directing. The suburban sex farce, a genre big in the mid-1960s, starred Robert Morse as a serial womanizer teaching his uptight neighbor, played by Walter Matthau, how to cheat on his wife (the curvaceous Inger Stevens). Kelly had recruited Art Carney, Lucille Ball, Jack Benny, Ben Blue, Terry-Thomas, Phil Silvers, Sid Caesar, and a host of others to make cameos in vignettes used by Morse's character to illustrate how *not* to get caught cheating on your wife.

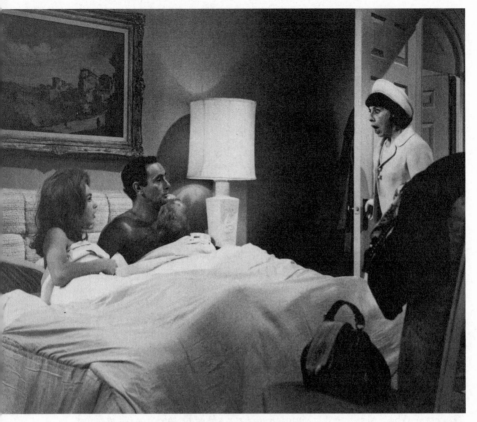

Charley (Joey) and his lady friend (Sharyn Hillyer) are caught in flagrante delicto *by Charley's wife (Ann Guilbert) in the funny "Deny, Deny, Deny" vignette from* A Guide for the Married Man (1967), *which also featured cameos from Jack Benny, Art Carney, Lucille Ball, and Phil Silvers (among others). (The Kobal Collection)*

Joey's vignette, the "Deny, Deny, Deny" scenario, was one of the film's highlights. Joey's character is caught in bed with another woman by his wife. He then proceeds to deny the entire incident ("What woman?") even as he and his girlfriend get dressed right in front of his wife—who begins to think she's imagining the whole thing.

"It's my first nude scene," Joey said. "I was terribly embarrassed. I never had met the girl before. Nobody introduced us until we got in bed together on the set."

Both *Who's Minding the Mint?* and *A Guide for the Married Man*
opened to positive reviews in early 1967, setting the table for the April
17 launch of *The Joey Bishop Show* on ABC. The network announced
in March that it was spending $2 million to renovate and "colorize"
its Vine Street studios, previously known as The Vine Street Theater.
Most of the ABC shows that had originated from the studio were
broadcast in black-and-white. Since *The Joey Bishop Show* would air in
color, newer, heavier lighting equipment was needed. ABC also pur-
chased four color cameras for the show and announced that Joey had
chosen Ray Charles and Danny Thomas as his first guests. Previous
reports that newlyweds Frank Sinatra and Mia Farrow would also be
on that first show turned out to be false, even though Joey remained
hopeful Sinatra would eventually make an appearance.

"It would be in a different light," he told a reporter. "It would
be just the two of us, center stage, with a single spot on us, and we'd
just talk. Did you know that Sinatra is quite a painter and one of his
paintings sold for $110,000 at a charity auction? That's the man I
want to bring on."

Joey also had definite ideas on how the show should be presented. "I wasn't looking to beat Carson, but I had what I thought
was a brilliant idea," he said. "It was based on having a two-piece
orchestra with no desk and an orange crate for a chair. I would be
threatening Johnny, 'I don't care how many musicians you got, if
you've got better music than this, I want to hear it.' Then two guys
would play. ABC agreed to this and then chickened out.

"I think it would have been hilarious, based on the thought
that a talk show is only as good as what people are saying the following morning about what happened the night before. That's the
secret of a talk show, 'My goodness, did you hear what so and so
said on Johnny last night?'"

The search for Joey's sidekick had landed a young TV host
named Regis Philbin, a native New Yorker and Notre Dame graduate who had been an NBC page for Steve Allen's *Tonight Show* in
the mid-1950s and was now hosting shows concurrently in San
Diego and in Hollywood. Philbin had succeeded Allen on Steve's
syndicated Westinghouse show, but that gig lasted only twenty
weeks and left a bitter taste in Philbin's mouth. Not wanting to get

burned again, Philbin initially told his agent not to pursue *The Joey Bishop Show* announcer/sidekick opportunity. But Philbin realized that the show, despite ABC's weak station lineup, would mean exposure to millions of people each weeknight. So Philbin drove to Los Angeles to meet with Joey, who had already interviewed dozens of people for the job. Philbin described the meeting in his memoirs, *I'm Only One Man!*

Joey was dressed casually, wearing an orange sweater, khaki pants, and his usual hangdog expression. Here was this official jester of the Sinatra Clan, the guy who kept Frank and Dean and Sammy laughing all those nights. I was intimidated, but he was very cordial and complimentary. He said, "I saw you with Joe Pyne last night and I enjoyed it. You have a talent" . . . So I said to Joey, "What talent? What's my talent?" And Joey literally rose to the occasion. He was a pretty good judge of ability and loved to express his opinions. So he stood up behind his desk, outlined against the window and paused to get his thoughts straight . . . It was quite a moment. Long, dramatic pause. Finally, Bishop said, "You are a good listener."

Joey told Philbin to go get a cup of coffee and come back in an hour. When Philbin returned, he found Joey surrounded by his agent, Norman Brokaw, his manager Ed Hookstratten, and Mel Bishop. In the time Philbin had been gone Joey's demeanor had changed; where he had been pleasant an hour before, his face was now beet-red, apparently after arguing with his inner circle over whether or not to hire Philbin.

Joey started right in on me now. There was no more cordiality. His staff had alarmed him. Suddenly, he wasn't so sure about me. He yelled out loud, "You had your own show! Now you're going to be the announcer! How do I know you're going to be content with that? How do I know you'll be able to sit there on the couch, night after night, without trying to butt in? How do I know you'll be able to keep your mouth shut?" he screamed. I stood up immediately, totally unfazed, and repeated back to him, "How do you know this? I'll tell you how you know. Because . . . I am a good listener!"

Joey was impressed. Philbin got the job.

CHAPTER

"He's a Real Mensch"

The Joey Bishop Show debuted on April 17, 1967, opposite very little late-night competition. Johnny Carson had walked off the Tonight Show two weeks earlier and was still embroiled in a contract dispute, trying to up his $15,000-a-week contract while arguing with NBC over Tonight Show rerun fees. While Carson sat it out, Jimmy Dean was filling in. That gave Joey an immediate edge, since it was reasoned many viewers would, at least, sample The Joey Bishop Show since Carson wasn't around. In addition to Danny Thomas and Ray Charles, Joey had invited newly elected California governor Ronald Reagan and actress Debbie Reynolds as his opening-night guests. Joey also poked some fun at the youthful Philbin by carrying out agent Norman Brokaw's young son, Joel, and introducing him to the audience as Regis.

But that was about all the fun Joey had that opening night. He looked uncomfortable behind his desk and fawned over his guests. It was something ABC hadn't expected from this show-biz veteran who despised phoniness and always lectured about "attitude." At one point, when Debbie Reynolds told Joey that she considered herself a tomboy, Joey turned to Regis. "Regis, why don't you just run across the stage?" he said. Philbin did as he was told and Reynolds ran after him, finally tackling him. Philbin later said he wondered if America, getting its first view of him that night, thought he was "a lightweight."

The critics had lauded Joey's pinch-hitting work for Paar and Carson, showering him with almost universal praise for his ability to

April 17, 1969: California governor Ronald Reagan was the first guest on The Joey Bishop Show. *(Courtesy ABC Photography Archives)*

counterpunch and ad-lib. But it was a different story once *The Joey Bishop Show* premiered.

Bob Williams, *The New York Post:* "Bishop may be quicker with the fast line than Carson, but he obviously isn't out to make any more sense on late-hour TV. Bishop introduced such guests as Danny Thomas, Debbie Reynolds, and a not-quite-ready newcomer songstress in what was a total imitation of the Carson-casts. Not a significant point was made, so to speak."

Jack Gould, *The New York Times:* "The spirited Miss Reynolds . . . was a welcome interlude of spontaneity, because otherwise Mr.

Bishop fell victim to the prevailing show business belief that a TV premiere event must be a ninety-minute credit crawl.

"Mr. Bishop is so effusive in his appreciation of his many warm and enduring acquaintances in Hollywood that his show bordered on sticky and dull banality. But he is too much of an intuitive showman to let that kind of corn continue. Separation of low-key modesty from overworked humility usually requires more than one show."

Harriet Van Horne: "One hesitates to 'Judge the play before the play be done,' but if the premiere of *The Joey Bishop Show* be taken as a token of things to come, Johnny Carson has nothing to worry about. There was a sense of strain—forgivable on an opening night—and a starchy uneasiness in the Joey Bishop opening . . . Though he's a quick wit and an able performer, he lacks the poise, the what-the-hell assurance that has distinguished all the successful night owl hosts—Steve Allen, Jack Paar, and the incumbent Carson."

Newsweek: "Seldom has an audience rocked with such noisy appreciation. Seldom had an opening show, even seen through the sentimental mist, fallen quite so flatly on the home screen."

The magazine also took a shot at Philbin, noting that the young co-host "acted as though he had walked through the wrong door and found himself onstage."

Despite the criticism, and no doubt helped by Carson's absence, the inaugural *Joey Bishop Show* won its time slot in New York, grabbing 41 percent of the audience compared to CBS's *"Late Show"* movie (24 percent) and the Jimmy Dean-hosted *Tonight Show* (12 percent).

That trend continued—for the rest of the week. Several days later, Carson ended his holdout and triumphantly announced that he would return to the *Tonight Show* on April 24. He was about $2 million richer and ready to battle his newest late-night foe.

Joey refused to take Carson's return sitting down and decided to call in a favor. He persuaded Jack Paar, who had been largely absent from the airwaves since 1962, to come out of semi-retirement. Joey wanted Paar as his guest for the April 24 show, which would be Carson's first night back on NBC. Joey's old pal and golfing buddy Buddy Hackett was booked for Carson's show that night and enraged Joey by telling the newspapers that Paar "will face a black screen for the first time in his life. I outdrew Paar when I was on his own show—and you can print that!"

Paar agreed to do *The Joey Bishop Show*, defending his decision by saying that Joey "was there" for him in 1961 when Paar was feuding with Ed Sullivan over guest fees and bookings. Paar added, however, that he had tried to persuade Joey from having him on the same night as Carson's return. "I wanted to go on later," he said.

"Joey, Jack, and I had a meeting in a hotel room the night before to talk about the show," said Hal Gurnee, Paar's former producer, who signed on for a thirteen-week stint directing *The Joey Bishop Show* until his next job kicked in. "This was around the Jewish holidays, and Joey's idea was that Jack would come out instead of Joey, the idea being that Joey couldn't be there after sundown.

"Jack didn't understand any of this and didn't want to be walking out there instead of Joey," Gurnee said. "He finally talked Joey out of it. He was also a little pissed that Joey was going to use him that way," to counteract Carson's return.

Either way, it didn't make a difference. Carson returned to thunderous applause and joked about his financial situation, likening it to the holiday of Passover, when Jews eat unleavened bread (matzoth). He said he "came back for more dough."

Meanwhile, *The Joey Bishop Show* that night could have been renamed *The Jack Paar Show*. Paar literally took the show over, to the point of sitting behind Joey's desk while Joey moved meekly to the guest's chair. Paar regaled the audience with anecdotes and even began interviewing guests Ethel Merman and Juliet Prowse (Sinatra's former fiancee). Joey, taken aback, could only utter "You'll have to forgive me for eavesdropping." He wasn't kidding.

"The elder statesman of late-night television so handily took command of the occasion's limited excitement that he inadvertently drew further attention to Mr. Bishop's plight as a host who is ill at ease in the presence of guests," sniffed *The New York Times*. Another critic noted that "Joey thought he had pulled a coup, but Paar's pulsating ego so dominated the evening that viewers were wondering who was doing whom a favor."

Despite Paar's re-emergence, *The Joey Bishop Show* was no match for Carson's return. In New York, *The Joey Bishop Show* finished a

Joey coaxed Jack Paar out of semi-retirement to appear on The Joey Bishop Show
in April 1967—the same night that Johnny Carson returned to The Tonight Show
*after a contract dispute. The stunt backfired when Paar literally took over the show—
even seating himself behind Joey's desk. (Courtesy ABC Photography Archives)*

distant fourth in its time slot with 12 percent of the audience. *The
Tonight Show,* meanwhile, snared a winning 41 percent, followed by
CBS's *Late Show* movie and Merv Griffin, who finished ahead of
Joey with 16 percent of the New York viewers.

The trend continued, as Carson regularly beat Joey in the ratings. By June, the *Tonight Show* held a 3 to 1 ratings margin over
The Joey Bishop Show, and whispers began that ABC was thinking of
canceling the show by mid-July. One report had ABC offering Joey

a buyout but keeping him with the network by negotiating a movie deal. Joey, meanwhile, complained vociferously in the press about the criticism of his show.

"Some of the members of the press who rapped me are the same ones who said I should have my own show after I pinch-hit for Carson a couple of times," he said. "Funny thing. People can forgive your mistakes when you pinch-hit. You don't have to be gracious when you're sitting in for somebody. But when you become host of your own show, then you have to combine graciousness with perseverance.

"I can't be anybody but me," he said. "It is the nature of this show that we set up a certain amount of hostility because we are a challenger—trying to prove we can put on as good a show as Carson. My biggest curse is being a performer, a stand-up comedian, which Paar, Carson, and Steve Allen weren't when they started this type of show."

But maybe there were other reasons that Joey's show wasn't working out as planned. "A lot of people had trouble getting along with Joey because he was pissed off most of the time—that's the impression I got while I was there," said Gurnee. "I found that to be funny about him; he would always be railing and ranting and pissed off, and he was funniest when he was doing that because he had these kind of bitter observations, which I found funny."

Joey brooded over the show's numbers, even when he was away from the Vine Street studio. Hours after taping *The Joey Bishop Show* he would sit in his Beverly Hills living room watching the show, scrutinizing his performance and critiquing his guests. He often invited that night's guest or guests back to Chevy Chase Drive to watch the show with him and have a snack.

"He would put the show on and watch it, mesmerized," said Mel Bishop. "Totie Fields did the show with him one night and Joey invited her back to the house with her husband, George. They got up, walked out, had something to eat and came back before the show was over. Joey never even knew they had left."

Regis Philbin, like everyone else around him, was subject to Joey's anger. But he also saw another side to his boss. Joey often told Regis that he considered him "a son," and shortly after the

Joey and Regis share an on-air smile, but behind the scenes of The Joey Bishop Show *the laughs were few and far between. (Courtesy ABC Photography Archives)*

show debuted, the boss and his sidekick started a daily practice of taking a mid-afternoon walk. They would chat with passersby and shoot the breeze, allowing Joey to calm down, clear his head, and prepare for that night's show. Philbin wrote about his daily walks with Joey in his memoirs.

At the stroke of three in the afternoon, we walked together. We would walk from 1313 North Vine Street all the way up to Hollywood Boulevard, all the way over to Cahuenga, all the way back down again. It took about fifty minutes, just long enough for Joey to clear his mind. And for me, it was a genuine pleasure, walking and talking with one of the masters, day after day, soaking up his knowledge. He told great show-business stories . . . Every day I learned something new, including how to treat fans and viewers. No matter how terrible a mood Joey was in, he'd be very gracious and cordial to everyone on the street.

Philbin had another reason to appreciate his boss. His future wife, Joy Senese, was working as Joey's secretary.

In early June, ABC surprised everyone by announcing that it was sticking with *The Joey Bishop Show* for its full thirty-nine-week run and perhaps beyond. "Nobody is born full-blown in this late-hour field," said network president Thomas W. Moore. "There is a high viewer-habit factor involved. You have to build slowly. We feel Joey Bishop is doing that—and we've advised him of our confidence."

Moore also denied reports the show was in the red. "We are well in the black," he said. If *The Joey Bishop Show* needed a further boost, it got one in August, when Joey interviewed David Janssen immediately following the highly touted finale of ABC's *The Fugitive*. In the much-hyped finale, Janssen's wrongly accused Dr. Richard Kimble finally came face-to-face with the one-armed man who had killed Kimble's wife.

Janssen appeared with Joey via split-screen, and *The Joey Bishop Show* that night grabbed a whopping 75 percent of the viewing audience in New York, topping Carson and the *Tonight Show* for the first time. It looked like Joey was finding his rhythm.

The show's ratings also started to pick up. Although Carson was still the champ, *The Joey Bishop Show* had closed the gap in the late-night talk show wars. By early 1968, Joey's show was averaging about 2.5 million viewers to Carson's 4 million viewers and had made substantial audience gains. ABC liked what it saw, and decided to renew *The Joey Bishop Show* for another year, taking Joey through January 1969. Since its premiere, ratings for *The Joey Bishop Show* had increased by roughly 40 percent and nineteen more ABC affiliates had signed up to carry the show, which was now seen on 146 ABC stations nationwide. That was still no match for Carson, who was on nearly 200 NBC stations, but it was a start.

ABC also discovered that viewers were beginning to sample *The Joey Bishop Show* and were liking what they saw. A technicians strike in September 1967 had forced Joey off the air for three weeks, and the public's reaction to his return could be measured in a sudden ratings spike. ABC decided to renew the show a month earlier than expected.

"It was really very good and we were doing very well," Joey said. "We were exceptionally strong in the Bible Belt, simply because I'm married to the same woman and I never drank."

The show was also adding new elements, including the team of Mark London and Jack Riley, who spoofed current events. London and Riley were hired by Joey after he saw them on Mort Sahl's local show on KTTV. Their tenure on *The Joey Bishop Show*, however, was short-lived. "We did it about ten times and then I think Joey became disenchanted with us," said Riley, who would later find fame as neurotic Mr. Carlin on *The Bob Newhart Show*. "Joey was kind of bitter, if I remember."

Bitter, maybe. But no one ever questioned Joey's loyalty to old friends and family. His older brother Morris, or "Moishe" as everyone called him, had moved to Los Angeles from Philadelphia in the 1950s and was working in the handbag business. As Joey had done for his brother Freddy, he included Moishe in his show-biz life, casting his big brother in an episode of *The Joey Bishop Show* in the early 1960s. Moishe was also a regular presence at the Vine Street Theater, where he had a front-row seat. One night, with Sammy Davis Jr. as his guest, Joey called Moishe up on stage for a soft-shoe number with Sammy.

"My father idolized Joey, absolutely idolized him," said Moishe's daughter, Marlene. "When Joey started coming out to California for various things, that's how they re-established a relationship. Joey would call my dad and dad would pick him up at the airport. Later in life they became much closer."

Joey also found time to schmooze on his talk show with his old comedy partner Rummy Bishop. Maybe Joey forgot their ill-fated conversation years before on *The Jack Paar Show*, when they had reminisced about the Bishop Brothers much to the bewilderment of the audience.

Even Joe Besser was, for a short while, back in the picture. After CBS cancelled *The Joey Bishop Show* in 1965, Besser was finding it hard, once again, to land a steady job. Joey, as he had done five years earlier, once again came to Besser's rescue, hiring him to be part of "The Son-of-a-Gun" players, a repertory group that provided comic relief for *The Joey Bishop Show* during its first season. Joining Besser in the group were Joanne Worley and Ann Elder. The "Son-of-a-Gun Players" would appear from behind one of four doors on the stage and engage in comic banter with Joey. The concept was later adapted for *Laugh-In*, the show that would make Worley a household name during that period. "I remember Dean Martin and Frank Sinatra considered our act their favorite part of the show," Besser later recalled.

Former Bishop Brother Mel Bishop rejoined Joey in the mid-1960s. Mel functioned as Joey's assistant and became part of the act as "The Messenger," delivering a telegram from Sands boss Jack Entratter regarding Joey's mandolin playing. (Courtesy Sands Hotel Collection, University of Nevada, Las Vegas Library)

But Joey's relationship with Mel Bishop was different in tone. Sure, the two men went back over thirty years to the old neighborhood in South Philly and their partnership in the Bishop Brothers. But Mel was now working *for* Joey—a situation that some people thought was a little odd and extremely awkward. Newspaper and magazine writers who profiled Joey in the late 1960s often seemed to be thunderstruck at the extent to which Mel catered to his boss, to the point of combing and spritzing Joey's transplanted hair and selecting his wardrobe.

TV Guide had profiled Joey often throughout the 1960s, often putting him on its cover during the run of the *Joey Bishop Show* sitcom. In February 1968, *TV Guide* ran a feature on *The Joey Bishop Show*, part of which detailed Mel's backstage duties.

Mel removes the wooden trees from Joey's black, wing-tipped shoes. From behind mirrored sliding doors, he selects one of sixty custom-made sports jackets, a double-vented number with built-up shoulders. "The sport outfit goes with the casualness of this kind of show," explains Bishop, adjusting a foulard handkerchief in his breast pocket. "I would feel more somber if I wore a suit. I would start to feel like I was dressed."

Joey pulls on a pair of black knee socks and a fresh blue suit. Mel hands him a pair of gray slacks, holding the legs off the carpeting so they will not attract lint . . . Joey adjusts his black tie . . . Mel anoints his head with hair spray. "We got a minute and a half," says Mel, handing his boss a shot glass of Scotch along with an ice-water chaser. He downs the whiskey in two quick sips, sighs and leaves for the studio. Backstage Bishop smokes one of the sponsor's cigarettes while Mel combs his bushy coiffure . . . Mel and Joey shake hands, just as they did before going on stage twenty-five years ago at places like Palumbo's in Philadelphia and the Casino Burlesque Theater in Pittsburgh. "Go get 'em," says Mel, completing the rite.

But Mel seemed to relish his job, and even thirty years later still talked enthusiastically, and without any bitterness, about his time spent with Joey.

"I did anything that came up that Joey shouldn't get mixed up in," he said. "It was nothing that important. I made sure the guests were ready, that they got in on time and that they were happy. I made sure the notes were there for the guests and I was in makeup, wardrobe, and lighting."

Joey and U.S. Army soldier Francisco Lopez during Joey's 10-day USO visit to Vietnam in 1968. (Courtesy Francisco Lopez)

Mel's duties also went beyond *The Joey Bishop Show*. He not only played a role in Joey's Vegas act but also kept the boss company and made sure Joey's public image was closely monitored. "Joey was a big tipper, not to make an impression, but he thought people had to make a living," Mel said. "I always made sure I had a lot of twenties and fives in my pocket when we went out, and I made damn sure that the people knew it wasn't my money."

Mel also accompanied Joey and Tippie Hedren on a ten-day USO tour of Vietnam in the fall of 1968.

"ABC wanted to turn it into some kind of documentary of what Joey was doing, and Joey said he didn't need that patriotism crap but ABC said they wouldn't sensationalize it," Mel said. "As soon as we got off the plane [the USO] put us on a patrol boat and took us down the Mekong River to a Marine base where no one had been for months or years. We were still wearing the same clothes from eighteen hours before, with the guys around us waiting to see if there would be sniper fire from the edge of the river.

"I tuned up a guitar, we got the kids around us, and we introduced Tippie Hedren, who had said she could sing. I hit the chord and she started to sing but then she got scared, so after that she went and visited orphanages. Joey and I went to bases that had been raided two hours before by the Viet Cong, places where [Bob] Hope and others wouldn't go. We went to Pearl Mountain—where we had the top and bottom and the Cong had the middle—and to a place where the guys were sitting there stoned, smoking grass."

Joey and Mel also threw out the USO rulebook and broke orders by flying in a chopper to greet some troops at a nearby base. Then, they took off as darkness fell. "The helicopter took off in the darkness and we saw flares going off," Mel said. "We were up there at 1,500 feet and suddenly we dropped. Joey grabbed a hold of me and we dropped to 500 feet. The USO raised hell with us. 'Don't you know what kind of predicament you put us in if you had gotten hurt?'"

When they arrived in Da Nang, Joey and Mel were greeted at their hotel by comedienne Martha Raye, who was working as a registered nurse on the front lines and had come by to say hello. "We were singing and raising hell there, and when Martha got back from Vietnam she came on Joey's show to talk about it," Mel said.

Joey would later cause something of a controversy when he lashed out at the USO in *Variety*. He complained that he had to leave from Seattle instead of Los Angeles, that there was no staff car to take him to the airport, and that performers were forced to go to Long Beach to get free shots.

"They make it so difficult," Joey said. "I've thought many times of going back, but then I've thought of all the trouble you have to go through. Anybody giving their time should be given some conveniences.

"It took fifteen calls to Washington to arrange things," he said. "In World War II, they had their tongues hanging out for anyone to come. Now it's like they do you a favor."

Joey's comments incurred the wrath of USO Council members George Jessel and actress Ann B. Davis ("Alice" on *The Brady Bunch*).

"I was there [in Vietnam] when Bishop was. He's a great performer, but all he did was shake hands," said Jessel. "The boys expect some entertainment."

"We're sorry he wasn't happy," said Davis. "It's so much easier to scream than to say something nice."

By mid-1968, *The Joey Bishop Show* had settled into a comfortable ratings groove. It was still lagging behind Carson's *Tonight Show*, and was drawing about 5 million viewers a night, to Carson's 7 million viewers. No one was confusing Joey for Johnny. But that was just as well, and actually worked to Joey's benefit. ABC researchers were discovering that Joey played better to middle-American audiences, who seemed to identify with his everyman persona. Carson, on the other hand, attracted a more urban audience with his more sophisticated brand of humor. Bill Dana's show was now history, and CBS had yet to enter the late-night fray, although it was still pursuing Merv Griffin.

ABC had also guessed, correctly, that *The Joey Bishop Show*'s proximity to Hollywood would draw big-name guests. Sinatra still hadn't agreed to visit Joey, although he had done *The Tonight Show*. But Sammy was a frequent guest, and even dropped by one night with Peter to chat about their new swingin'-in-London movie, *Salt and Pepper*. That was the night that Joey and Regis wore Nehru jackets in their attempt to imitate Sammy's hip dress code. Dean also dropped by the show several times, telling anyone who would listen that Joey's eight-minute opening monologue with Regis was the best thing on television.

Joey had never been able to find his groove on the sitcom, which had begun disastrously and improved only slightly over time. But that show had only been on the air once a week. Back in the spring of 1967, when he had met with the ABC affiliates to help sell his talk show, Joey had promised that *The Joey Bishop Show*, given time to grow and develop, would offer an alternative to Johnny Carson and the *Tonight Show*.

And now that the ratings began to improve, Joey was beginning to look like a genius. Sure, it was grueling doing ninety minutes a night, five nights a week. But the airtime, and ABC's willingness to stick with the show, allowed Joey the luxury of finding his rhythm. For starters, he had toned down his fawning over the guests after those first few disastrous weeks. Always an avid reader interested in current events, Joey began steering his show toward social issues like gun control (with guests Charlton Heston and Hugh O'Brian), civil rights (which he discussed with Charles Evers and Marlon Brando), and Vietnam, which became a frequent topic as the war raged on and President Lyndon Johnson announced his decision not to seek a second term. The fact that Joey, and not Carson, had traveled to Southeast Asia to see the troops lent credibility to his views on Vietnam. It also went a long way toward explaining the differences between the two men.

Issues and answers: Joey chats up GOP presidential candidate Richard Nixon on The Joey Bishop Show *(1968). (ABC Photography Archives)*

Where Carson might only joke about current events in his monologue, Joey engaged his guests in thoughtful discussions. Former vice president Richard Nixon, who was now running for president, stopped by to chat about his campaign. Nixon's appearance was matched by his two opponents, former vice president Hubert Humphrey and Senator Eugene McCarthy, who was running as an Independent. Joey even tossed actor Pernell Roberts off the show one night after a heated exchange about America's involvement in Vietnam.

Tears were also not an uncommon occurrence on *The Joey Bishop Show*. Actor George Raft broke down while discussing his career woes, and comedian Redd Foxx, who had battled racism for years, lost his composure while describing his struggle to break into the "mainstream" comedy world. Joey got his pal Buddy Hackett to admit to a four-year marijuana habit, which he said he had since kicked because "you live in a gray world." Bing Crosby's son, Gary, who had appeared with Joey in *Sergeants 3,* came on *The Joey Bishop Show* and told America he was an alcoholic.

Even reclusive actor Marlon Brando came on the show one night, just a few weeks after police in Oakland, California, had shot and killed a seventeen-year-old Black Panther named Bobby Hutton. Brando described Hutton's death as "a shootout with police," telling Joey that Hutton came out of his house with his hands up and "was shot down in front of any number of witnesses." Three Oakland cops, who were watching Brando on *The Joey Bishop Show,* sued him for slander.

Joey even received an angry telegram from a Harlem minister after having segregationist George Wallace on the show for a half-hour interview. Rev. A. Kendall Smith, representing the Ad Hoc Committee for the Anti-Wallace-LeMay demonstration, wrote, "We are inclined to believe and are disappointed that Mr. Bishop has given aid and comfort to Mr. Wallace. While being a minister of the Gospel and an advocate of compassion, I feel that . . . Mr. Bishop was overly compassionate."

TV Guide, which was one of Joey's biggest boosters over the years, featured Joey on its cover in early March 1968. That cover turned out to be the magazine's best-selling issue ever (14.6 million copies) up to that point. Even the old gray lady of newsmagazines,

Newsweek, took notice of Joey's show, running a full-page article entitled "The Kid from Philly."

While Johnny projects a detached, witty sophistication, Joey makes his audience care—and even cry occasionally. Whether agonizing over a guest's problems or painfully groping through a sermon on the need for more human kindness, he is a real Mensch—or what the hippies call "out front" with no defenses . . . The approach may appear tastelessly gooey to some viewers, but it seems to work a special effect on guests.

Behind-the-scenes, though, the situation was anything but rosy. ABC seemed pleased with Joey and with the show's direction and had extended Joey's contract through mid-October 1969. The network was even saving about $800,000 a year when it decided to tape *The Joey Bishop Show* a day in advance, rather than airing it live, which involved satellite uplink fees and other costs. And ABC certainly couldn't complain about the show's ratings, which had risen steadily to the point where, by April 1968, a year after its inauspicious debut, *The Joey Bishop Show* was regularly pulling in 23 percent of the late-night audience. Carson was averaging 26 percent of that audience, making Joey's feat all-the-more impressive since *The Joey Bishop Show* was seen on about fifty less stations than Carson's *Tonight Show.*

Joey's sidekick Regis Philbin, however, was another story. Almost from day one, ABC executives had pressured Joey to fire Philbin. The feeling among ABC brass was that Philbin was somehow bringing the show down, though no one could specifically say *how.* Joey, however, vehemently resisted the push to fire Philbin and find someone else. He liked Philbin and enjoyed their daily constitutionals up Vine Street. And he thought Philbin brought a youthful exuberance to the show.

"Everybody keeps telling me [to fire him] and I keep defending him," Joey said of Philbin. "In fact, a while back, I went to a convention of the affiliates—there were 200 station managers there—and every one of them said the same thing: 'When are you going to get rid of Regis?'

"But I'm not going to, and I told the network that," he said. If he goes, I go. Listen, I think he's doing a good job."

Sure, there had been several hiccups, like the time Philbin shared some fan mail with a Chicago newspaper reporter, who printed a few

Joey and Regis take in the sights on their daily stroll up Vine Street. (ABC Photography Archives)

of the letters. One of the letters asked Regis "why you put up with the snide attack by the egotistical, ignorant, and piggish . . . " Joey figured the dot-dot-dot referred to "Jew," although he knew the letter writer wasn't referring to him but to another comedian. Still, Joey went ballistic over the fact that Regis had given that particular letter to the reporter. When Philbin visited Chicago several months later, Joey gave the direct order—no press interviews for Regis.

Philbin knew that he was a marked man, that ABC executives weren't happy with his performance. He also knew that Joey, who never mentioned any of this to Regis, had continued to go to bat for him. Regis finally shared his frustration with Joey in early July 1968, during their daily walk up Vine Street.

Joey and Regis Philbin in front of the Vine Street Theatre during one of their daily walks. (Courtesy ABC Photography Archives)

"Do you think it's me?" I asked Joey. "Should I quit? If you think I'm hurting the show, I'll go." Joey gave me a surprised look. "No, I don't think it's you," he said evenly. But I saw a little light go off in his eyes. Coincidence or not, we both knew that the following week Johnny Carson would be bringing the Tonight Show out to NBC's facilities in Burbank, our own backyard. Whenever Carson came West, it was a big event and his ratings soared. Joey, for his part, hated network politics and didn't much like his ABC bosses, especially the ones who wanted my blood. So he said to me, "I'll tell you a way to get back at them. Why don't you—only if you feel like it—walk off one night? Walk off right on the air, like Jack Paar used to do. You'll *show them." Then he said, "Just know that if you walk, I'll make sure you come back."*

The seed had been planted. Although by Philbin's account Joey hadn't directly told him to walk off the show, he did seem to suggest that it would be a huge publicity stunt, one that could help the show and steal Carson's thunder. And what would be the harm? After all, Joey would bring Regis back, and *that* show could also be a big ratings draw. It had worked for Jack Paar, right? What did they have to lose?

Mel Bishop remembers the situation a little differently.

"It was Joey's idea, he set it up," he said of Philbin's walkout. "ABC wanted Regis off the show; they thought he was hurting the show and they wanted a change. Joey said to Regis, 'When we go on, I want you to tell the audience that this is a wonderful experience and you love everything that's going on, but you feel you're a detriment to the show and you think you're holding the show back and you don't want to do that. So, for the betterment of the show, you're going to leave. And you'll walk off.'"

And so he did. On July 11, Carson's first night in town, Regis gave Joey his customary introduction and walked over to where Joey stood, ostensibly to begin their jokey eight-minute monologue. Here's Philbin's account of what happened next:

I walked over to him, as usual. Except I didn't give him the usual pep talk. Instead, I started slowly. "I have something to say to you," I told him. "I've wanted to say it all day. I'm leaving this show." Joey looked stunned, like I'd hit him with a plank. I turned to the audience and said, "Joey hired me against everybody's better judgment—including the network's. Today I overheard something that disturbed me. I heard that for fifteen months they've been on his back because of me. So I'm quitting." Joey struggled to make a joke: "Don't leave me," he said, "because they'll find out that it was me hurting the show instead of you!" ... But I went on: "Maybe I'm wrong for the show, maybe I'm holding you back, maybe we could do better without me here. They all could be right. So I tell you what—I'm going to go. I'm leaving."

As the audience audibly gasped, Philbin walked off the stage, passing singer Vic Damone on the way out and disappearing into the night.

The papers had a field day with the walkout. One report even had Philbin weeping in his dressing room before leaving the studio (that never happened). "Regis Philbin staged a Jack Paar exit last night on *The Joey Bishop Show* following an emotional eight-minute tirade about the network not being satisfied with his performance," Kay Gardella wrote in the *New York Daily News*. "Bishop, when contacted by this reporter, called his program a nighttime version of *Peyton Place*. He predicted that Philbin would be back, but admitted he did not show up for yesterday's taping . . . Bishop was as shocked by Philbin's actions as was the network and TV audience."

Joey continued to insist to the press that he knew nothing of Philbin's planned walkout. ABC, angry at Philbin's actions, issued a statement the next day. "ABC is surprised at the action and statements made by Regis Philbin on *The Joey Bishop Show* Thursday, July 11. We feel that his statements were unwarranted and had no basis in fact. When ABC executives met with Joey Bishop today, Joey said 'Regis is a fine but sensitive young man and everything is going to be fine.'"

The drama continued for several days, as Philbin laid low and evaded the press. Musical director Johnny Mann filled in for Philbin the rest of the week, introducing Joey and bantering with his boss. ABC, meanwhile, was being blitzed with letters, telegrams and phone calls from viewers pleading for Regis to come back. That weekend, according to Philbin, Joey called. "It's time to come back," he said.

I must have hedged a little, since I was still shaken up by the fact that rumors had circulated in the first place. Joey said, "If you don't come back, you'll be hurting no one but me. I need you." And I could tell that he meant it.

Philbin returned the following Monday, one week after walking off the show. The publicity stunt, if indeed that's what it was, had worked, for the time being.

The popularity of *The Joey Bishop Show* was enough to convince Joey, or some genius at ABC Records, to follow in the footsteps of *Star Trek* star William Shatner and cut an album. Shatner had croaked out his interpretations of several pop tunes, including his unforgettable rendition of The Beatles classic "Lucy in the Sky with Diamonds" and

The Rhinestone Cowboy: Joey as he appeared on the album cover of Joey Bishop Sings Country and Western. *(Courtesy ABC Photography Archives)*

Bob Dylan's "Mr. Tambourine Man," which Howard Stern would use to comic effect years later on his radio show. Joey, however, took another approach to his hot-wax debut. Hal Gurnee, who had helped launch *The Joey Bishop Show*, discovered he shared a love of country music with Joey and had booked many country-and-western acts on the show (Joey said he liked their "honesty"). Joey took it one step further, and actually cut an album of country-and-western tunes on ABC Records, the network's in-house label.

Joey Bishop Sings Country and Western featured Joey on its cover, sporting a garish, blue-suede cowboy outfit complete with white Stetson hat and boots. The album included songs like "It Keeps Right On a Hurtin'," "Take These Chains from My Heart," "Heartbreak Avenue," and "Your Cheatin' Heart." It went absolutely nowhere (and hasn't yet been discovered by Howard Stern). Regis Philbin didn't fare much better. He, too, released a forgettable album called *It's Time For Regis!* after a Mercury Records executive saw him crooning "Pennies from Heaven" to Bing Crosby on *The Joey Bishop Show.*

Joey Signs Off

The year 1969 would be known for many historic developments. Neil Armstrong's first steps on the moon. The Amazin' Mets. Woodstock. The Tate–LaBianca murders.

Merv Griffin.

Okay, so Merv Griffin wasn't exactly pivotal to world events in 1969, but he was pivotal to Joey Bishop's career. CBS, which had sat out the late-night talk show game, finally hired Griffin away from Group W in August 1968 after flirting with Jack Paar. Griffin's national show was scheduled to premiere in September 1969, from New York, in the ninety-minute timeslot opposite the *Tonight Show* and *The Joey Bishop Show*. Griffin's Group W show had proven to be somewhat of a spoiler in New York, where it often beat *The Joey Bishop Show*. CBS liked what it saw of Griffin, a former Big Band singer who oozed personality and had his own sidekick in British actor Arthur Treacher. The network signed Griffin to a six-year contract that would pay him $1 million a year.

The news of Griffin's entrance into the late-night arena was somewhat alarming to ABC. Although Joey's show had seemed to find its niche and was, by all accounts, making money for the network ($11 million a year, by most estimates), the ABC affiliates were beginning to grumble. Joey's ratings had stalled, and by the time Griffin launched his show, *The Joey Bishop Show* had lost about forty affiliates. That meant it was being aired on only 125 stations. Griffin, meanwhile, was launching on 152 stations.

There were already whispers that ABC executives were considering dropping Joey, who was signed through January 1971 but was quickly losing sponsors as his ratings dipped. Dick Cavett had hosted a thrice-weekly summer show on ABC and was rumored to be a possible (cheaper) replacement. But his ratings hadn't been much better.

Joey, for his part, didn't sound too concerned about the new competition from Griffin.

"I said the same thing when I went on—the viewers are the ones to benefit from this," he told *The New York Times*. "When you get competition you work just a little harder. If you're the only craps player in town you play the odds you want. Each one of us will be putting on our thinking caps as to how we can use our guests best."

Carson, who knew he had nothing to fear, was equally nonplussed about Griffin's show. "I don't know what it means," he said. "That's what I said when Joey went on the air."

ABC's worst fears were realized soon after *The Merv Griffin Show* launched and began to slowly pick up steam in the ratings department. Carson's *Tonight Show* was still unbeatable, and was averaging about 35 percent of the late-night TV audience. But by November, just a short time after its debut, *The Merv Griffin Show* was pulling in 19 percent of the audience. *The Joey Bishop Show*, meanwhile, lagged in a distant third with 13 percent of American TV viewers. "We had a strange thing happen," Joey said. "When I was on ABC, CBS was also showing my show on some of its stations, and then Merv Griffin came along and those affiliates went back to CBS."

The writing was on the wall, and ABC didn't wait much longer to pull the plug. On November 24, 1969, it broke the news to Joey that it was canceling *The Joey Bishop Show* at the end of December.

"My agent and manager came in at 4 P.M. and said ABC is canceling you," Joey said. "They said, you have a choice: You can stay on until the end of November or you can leave and choose who you'd like to replace you."

Joey waited until the next day, during his monologue, to tell his stunned audience that he and ABC decided to end the show "for multiple reasons." Alluding to Carson and Griffin, Joey went on to

November 25, 1969: Joey calls it quits, announcing that The Joey Bishop Show *has been cancelled before abruptly walking off and turning the show over to Regis Philbin.*

say that *The Joey Bishop Show* didn't have the ratings to stay "in this kind of three-way race."

"I asked ABC for a little time off, but this is ridiculous," he joked. "It was one hell of a good battle," he said. "I am proud of all the talent, co-workers and staff that worked terribly hard to make it a success for two-and-a-half years."

Joey praised his staff some more ("They gave it everything") and then paused. "If I want to say more I'll get Johnny or Merv to let me on to say it," he proclaimed, then announced to America that he was going home to have dinner with his wife and turned the show over to Regis Philbin. It was all over in a matter of fifteen minutes.

As he walked off the stage, Joey passed guest Vic Damone backstage. A year-and-a-half earlier, Damone had been backstage when Philbin walked off the show. Show-business karma.

Two days later, ABC named Dick Cavett as Joey's replacement. The network said that it wasn't sure if Joey would return to finish his final weeks on the show (he didn't). Jan Murray, Norm Crosby, and a host of others filled in the next few weeks until Cavett could get his late-night team in place. "When ABC cancelled Joey's show they told him it was due to poor ratings. The only problem was that that Joey realized that all their shows were doing poorly, relatively speaking, and his was doing well," said Crosby. "So he walked off the show before his contract ran out. The network called me to ask if I'd fill in until the end of the season, since I'd made several appearances on the show. When I told them no they seemed surprised that a person wouldn't jump at the chance to host a network show, but I just didn't want to do that to Joey and would only do it if he asked me himself. The network told me it was his suggestion that I take over but I still needed to hear it from him. When he called me to tell me that he gave me his blessing to do it, I then filled in and finished up *The Joey Bishop Show* in its final season."

"I'm shocked, really, by the TV editors," Joey said in an interview shortly after the cancellation. "Usually they can smell out a story. How come nobody asked how ABC could sign me for an extra year and then drop me only four months later?

"Did anyone compare my ratings and Dick Cavett's?" he said, taking a shot at his successor. "How come the show was given to someone who had already failed three times—in the morning and in prime time? How many chances does one guy get? What were they trying to prove?"

He then went on to blame his sponsors, and his choice of guests, for the show's cancellation.

"For me, I guess it was only a matter of time, anyhow. When the anti-smoking campaign began, I refused to hold up a package of cigarettes, because kids nine, ten years old were writing letters.

"I don't think that went over too well with ABC, but who knows? I was warned of the penalties if I got involved in the drug thing, because one of the show's sponsors was a big pharmaceutical company.

"I was never censored, but I thought certain guests should be heard [that] they thought were too dull. I say this very proudly, when I got cancelled after two years and nine months, the next week I signed a contract to replace Johnny Carson for six weeks a year. So how badly could I have been doing?"

Joey said he wasn't bitter, and maybe he wasn't. After all, ABC's buyout was generous—it was reported to be $1.2 million over ten years—and Joey still had the nightclub act, which was going great guns in Vegas, Tahoe, and Miami Beach. Shortly after he left ABC, Joey received a call from his old pal Dave Tebet, over at NBC, who asked Joey to fill in for Johnny on the *Tonight Show*. Joey even went out and bought a twenty-five-foot speedboat he nicknamed "Son of a Gun," which he kept docked at Marina del Rey.

But Joey had been a television fixture for ten years, going back to the *Keep Talking* days and those halcyon nights with Jack Paar. His sitcom might have been a throwback to a certain era, but it had lasted four seasons—an eternity in the ephemeral television landscape. And the talk show had given Joey a certain relevance, with its emphasis on social issues and topical discussion. Now, that too, was gone. Joey's relationship with Sinatra was virtually non-existent now, Sammy was doing his own thing, and Dean was turning into the boozer he had parodied for so many years. Peter, meanwhile, was chasing girls half his age and battling various addictions. Age was beginning to catch up to all of them.

Joey had sworn off doing the club circuit years before, when the TV work was abundant and the movie scripts were rolling in. He was fifty-two now and he didn't need the money, or the aggravation, of working up new material.

But what else was he going to do?

For starters, he became more immersed in his charity work. For years, Joey had been involved in helping raise money for different causes, including the Leukemia Society in Philadelphia and a foundation started by TV star Chuck Connors, who headlined ABC's *The Rifleman*.

"Chuck Connors had a little facility in Palm Springs that took care of disabled children and he came on [*The Joey Bishop Show*] and spoke to Joey about it," said Mel Bishop. "Joey made it his business that he was going to help, and he would gather up as many friends as he could and once or twice a year raise money for Connors' foundation."

Throughout the 1960s Joey had hosted several telethons, including one for the Philadelphia Variety Club (again benefiting handicapped children). In 1968, at the height of his fame, he even insisted on paying his own way back to Philadelphia to host a benefit for the Sons of Italy.

And then there was St. Luke's and Children's Medical Center, a facility on Girard Avenue in Philadelphia that was run by Dr. James Giuffre, with whom Joey struck up a close friendship beginning in 1967.

Joey became interested in the hospital's drug rehabilitation program, run by Dr. Giuffre, and had contributed $75,000 to maintain the program's drug rehab facilities. He visited St. Luke's whenever he was in Philly, stopping by to chat with the drug-addicted patients and to spend some time with Giuffre. Insiders at the hospital knew that Joey even paid some patients' hospital bills, without ever once publicizing his acts of kindness.

Joey's bond with Dr. Giuffre was so strong, and his belief in the drug-rehab program so unbreakable, that he went to great lengths to keep the program afloat. Joey even attended a Philadelphia zoning board meeting on Dr. Giuffre's behalf to support a proposed plan for an addicts' halfway house in Fox Chase. In February 1970, St. Luke's dedicated the "Joey Bishop Try a Little Kindness Lounge" in his honor. Nine years later, the lounge grew into The Joey Bishop Addictive Disease Center, its expansion funded largely by money Joey had helped to raise.

The performing now, such as it was, seemed almost secondary to Joey. But in March 1970, still smarting from the ABC cancellation, Joey announced he would begin a new nightclub tour that summer, backed by fellow Philly comics Al Fisher and Lou Marks. He warmed up by reuniting with Mel Bishop and Rummy Bishop at The Log Cabin in Philly and worked out the kinks up in Vancouver at The Cave. In August, Joey opened at The Sands before a star-studded crowd including Johnny Carson, Sammy Davis Jr., George Burns, Louis Prima, and Sonny King.

The old magic was still there, at least in Vegas. The crowds were less sophisticated and, perhaps, less in tune with the pointed, urban comedy now making itself heard through socially hip comedians like Richard Pryor and George Carlin. Nobody who came to The Sands to see Joey Bishop expected to hear about drugs or racial strife.

But it was especially cruel that Joey's revitalized nightclub career, which was so promising in Las Vegas, would crash and burn in his own backyard. In November 1970, Joey opened at the Latin Casino in Cherry Hill, N.J. before a large crowd composed mostly of Philadelphians. Al Fisher, Lou Marks, and Mel Bishop were along for support—both comedic and emotional.

Joey's first week at The Latin Casino went smoothly. The newspapers gave Joey generally good reviews, and the crowds were impressive. "Maybe some people can never go home again, but Joey Bishop made it clear that he can come back any time he so desires," enthused *The Philadelphia Inquirer*. "There's sure to be a party." *The Philadelphia Daily News*, however, said that Joey was "lacking in sparkle" and saved its biggest raves for Mel Bishop ("igniting the homecoming crowd") and "vibrant" singer Gerri Granger.

Then, on November 15, about a week into Joey's two-week engagement, disaster struck. A group of hecklers began razzing Joey just seconds after he appeared on stage. Joey was shocked at the reception and walked off in a huff, demanding that the hecklers be removed from the club. He returned to the stage a short time later, apologized to the audience, and began to speak when the loudest heckler started in again. "If he stays, I leave," Joey announced. Well, he stayed, and Joey left. He walked off the Latin Casino stage and headed back to the Bellevue Stratford Hotel in Philly. Joey made sure the customers, who waited an hour for him to return, were given refunds. But he was obviously embarrassed and angry at his rude reception. This was Philadelphia, after all. If they didn't love him here, well . . .

"I don't mind hecklers, but this heckler and his friends had no intention of making the show a show," Joey said. It was whispered that the hecklers were plants, that Joey was "irked" by the small crowds and was trying to drum up business by making some headlines.

If Joey was looking for more publicity he certainly found it when he cancelled the rest of The Latin Casino engagement. The next day, Joey checked himself into St. Luke's under the care of Dr. Giuffre. The diagnosis: exhaustion.

"We don't expect to find anything serious," Giuffre said. "Joey needs a break in his routine. The fact that he consented to go into the hospital is an indication that he really feels rotten. I think he will snap back in two or three days. Joey kept going because he felt he had an obligation to his public. He was not getting any relaxation . . . He hasn't been eating properly and has dropped too much weight."

For all intents and purposes, The Latin Casino disaster marked the end of Joey's career playing the smaller clubs. Over the next few years he would play several small club dates, but his days of touring with a nightclub act were over. He now limited himself to the bigger venues in Vegas and Atlantic City, which continued to pay top dollar for Joey Bishop. He didn't need the aggravation, and he was financially sound, so he could pick and choose when and where he wanted to work. And NBC had been in touch, asking Joey if he was available to pinch-hit for Johnny Carson on an as-needed basis. After thirty-plus years in the business, Joey was beginning to slow down.

Joey was booked to guest-host for Carson on the *Tonight Show* in April 1971, but he was called into duty a month early when Carson developed a case of mild hepatitis and was hospitalized for two weeks. The *Tonight Show* marked Joey's first late-night appearance, of any kind, since his walking off *The Joey Bishop Show* a year-and-a-half earlier. His return to the late-night arena, albeit as a guest host, made headlines. Joey insisted he wasn't interested in replacing Carson on a permanent basis, if Johnny's health became a chronic problem.

"I did it two years and eight months night after night on ABC. I don't think I could do it again," he told *New York Post* columnist Earl Wilson. "I faced it with the wrong attitude. You just have to laugh at it. Johnny can do that. I always say I'm constantly helping Johnny. I helped him when I had my own show by *having* my own show."

And there were some more changes coming down the pike. In 1972, Joey and Sylvia sold the mansion on Chevy Chase Drive in Beverly Hills and moved to a smaller place down the road in Newport Beach. It was right on the water, with a beautiful view of the setting sun, and had a bay window overlooking the dock where Joey moored his boat.

The decreased workload meant that there was less for Mel Bishop to do for Joey. He decided to call it quits soon after Joey and Sylvia moved to Newport Beach. "It meant I couldn't come out to the house every day and work on things," Mel said. "So I said, 'Let's leave on good terms. There's no reason for me to stay here and pick up a salary.' So we cooled it. I saw him a few times after that." After leaving Joey, Mel hooked up with impressionist Rich Little, a job he held for about fifteen years. Little's wife, like Joy Philbin, had once worked as Joey's secretary.

Joey was still commanding $75,000 a week in Vegas, where he continued to appear semi-regularly. But he was now more interested in cruising on his boat, *Sonuvagun II*, than in performing on stage. Joey became a member of the Coast Guard Auxiliary, and his boating prowess made headlines in 1972, when twice within three weeks he rescued boaters who were stranded off the coast of Marina del Rey.

Exit, Stage Left

A s the 1970s progressed, Joey became less and less of a presence on television, the medium that had launched his career. Notwithstanding his guest-hosting gigs on the *Tonight Show*, Joey relegated himself to game shows (*The Match Game*, *Celebrity Sweepstakes*, *Liar's Club*), some guest-starring roles on series *(Chico and the Man)* and the occasional appearance on one of Dean Martin's *Celebrity Roast* specials for NBC. He talked about syndicating a television show to spotlight new talent, but the project never got off the ground. Joey got together with Arthur Marx (Groucho's son) to write his memoirs, but that project also stalled and was eventually forgotten. "I only knew him [Joey] casually," Marx said. "We were going to do a book together about Sinatra. We met three or four times and I did an outline, but he said, 'You know what, I don't think Frank would be happy with this.'"

Unwittingly, however, Joey became the topic of a sketch on NBC's *Saturday Night Live*, which began in 1975 and quickly gained a (well-deserved) reputation as one of the most original sketch-comedy shows in television history.

In the sketch, which was written by Matt Neuman, Don Novello (who also played "Father Guido Sarducci"), and Alan Zweibel, a couple (Bill Murray and Gilda Radner) invites their neighbors (Richard Benjamin and Paula Prentiss) over to their house for the first time. After a few minutes, the couples find that they have nothing to talk about. Desperate for a conversation-starter, the character played by Benjamin spots an ashtray on the coffee table.

"Hey, is this from the Sahara in Las Vegas?" he asks. "Yeah, we go there every year, to see Joey," responds Murray's character. "Joey? You mean Joey Bishop? We love Joey too!" says Benjamin, relieved to have something to talk about. The two couples, finding a common thread, then begin an animated discussion about Joey, talking about his movies ("He was the best thing about *Texas across the River!*") and Regis Philbin ("the traitor").

"We always go to the early shows," says Prentiss, when the talk turns to Joey's performances at the Sahara. "Joey's always better at the early show." "What do you mean he's better?" says Murray. "We go to the late show. He's looser at the late show."

"Yeah, we always go to the late show," says Radner. "He's much looser." And, with that, the conversation degenerates, as the couples argue about the merits of the "early show" Joey versus the "late show" Joey, with Benjamin and Prentiss eventually storming out of the house.

Meanwhile, the real Joey Bishop could still pick a fight. He erupted in the newspapers when talk-show host Mike Douglas moved his show out of Philadelphia and took a parting shot at the locals as people who "would probably boo Santa Claus in a Christmas parade." "Mike is about as sincere as Zsa Zsa Gabor yelling 'ouch' on her wedding night," Joey shot back. Another time, he argued so much with Al Martino over their billing at a Philadelphia-sponsored street show that Martino finally dropped out altogether to avoid the headache.

Joey and Sylvia became grandparents when Larry's daughter was born in 1975. That same year, Joey returned to Philadelphia to play two-and-a-half weeks at Palumbo's, where he had gotten his start nearly forty years before with The Bishop Brothers. Joey had called owner Frank Palumbo from Newport Beach, requesting the booking and inadvertently throwing Palumbo into a tizzy. Would Joey command the same $75,000-a-week salary he was pulling down in Vegas? (Joey's response: "Listen, if I were worried about money, would I want to work in South Philadelphia?")

It had been five years since the Latin Casino incident, but this time there were no hecklers and no walkouts, and the Palumbo's gig went smoothly. A year later, in November 1976, Joey returned to

Palumbo's, telling jokes about his Newport Beach neighbor John Wayne ("He's got a Japanese gardener. He doesn't have a garden. But twice a day the gardener surrenders") and opening for Danny Thomas in Vegas ("It's not often a Jew goes out to help an Arab in the desert"). He reprised the bongo bit and the waiter bit that he used to do with Mel Bishop, with Gene Arcade now playing the waiter. Joey even whipped out the old mandolin.

Joey also re-teamed with Danny Thomas for a tour of smaller venues, including the Valley Forge Music Fair outside of Philadelphia. Both men had apparently smoothed over whatever differences they had from the old *Joey Bishop Show* days, when Thomas had thrown up his hands in disgust and handed the production reins over to Eddie Rio.

"As Joey explained it last night, no one can top the Lebanese master of song and comedy. So true to form, Bishop opened the show last night at the Valley Forge Music Fair where the pair are teamed in a boisterous evening of pure entertainment at its best," read a review in *The Philadelphia Bulletin*. "Thomas, relaxed and at ease with the definitely partisan audience, takes his fans on a nostalgic trip with song and story back to the 'old days' . . . the quick-witted Bishop seemed to be 'winging it' as the show went along but this appearance surely comes from the mastery of his craft which was rewarded by two standing ovations from the crowd."

In August 1979, Joey landed at Resorts International in Atlantic City for a three-week run opposite Luce Ennis in *The Mind with the Dirty Man*, a sex farce about a middle-aged businessman (played by Joey) who wages a war against smut in a small New Jersey town. The role was a familiar one for Joey; several years earlier, in Chicago, he and Larry had co-starred in the same play.

Larry had pursued an acting career after graduating from Beverly Hills High, and had snagged small roles in several TV series *(I Dream of Jeannie, The Mothers-in-Law)* and in low-budget movies *(Wild in the Streets, The Savage Seven, Angel Unchained)*. But Larry never did become became a star like his high school pals Richard Dreyfuss, Albert Brooks, and Rob Reiner. While Dreyfuss was winning an Oscar for *The Goodbye Girl* and Reiner was starring as Mike "Meathead" Stivic on *All in the Family*, Larry was toiling in small roles on shows like *Barney Miller, Laverne & Shirley,* and *Dukes of Hazzard* and in small movie roles *(C.H.O.M.P.S., The Sting II)*.

In the meantime, Joey was plotting his television comeback. He had devised a show called *Joey Bishop Super TV Bingo.* Joey would host the daytime show, in which a studio audience and viewers at home would play a version of bingo, with cards supplied by local supermarkets.

Joey and his partner, Ben Miller, had shopped the show through their production company, Bishop–Miller Productions. Group W had shown interest in airing the show live in Philadelphia—ironically, from the same studio that housed *The Mike Douglas Show.* Stations in New York, Baltimore, Pittsburgh, San Francisco, Boston, and Charlotte, North Carolina, were expected to sign up. Joey would be paid $7,500 a week for the first five stations and an additional $1,000 a week from any additional stations that signed up to air the show. He confidently predicted that *Joey Bishop Super TV Bingo* would be aired on 200 stations nationwide—about fifty more ABC stations than had ever aired *The Joey Bishop Show.* Joey was excitedly about his new project and even talked about moving back to Philadelphia permanently.

But *Joey Bishop Super TV Bingo* wasn't to be. Just days after announcing plans for the show, which was reportedly scheduled to debut in January 1981, Joey said investors had been "overly exuberant" in their predictions for the show's launch date. He now said he didn't expect an answer on the show's future until February or later. Like his planned TV talent show and his memoirs, *Joey Bishop Super TV Bingo* quietly withered and died on the vine.

But those projects were nothing compared to the last act in Joey Bishop's long career: Broadway.

Even during the height of his fame in the mid-1960s, Joey could only have dreamed about starring in a Broadway show. But it was about to become a reality. Mickey Rooney had stunned everyone by revitalizing his career as the star of *Sugar Babies,* a burlesque review co-starring Ann Miller. The show rode a wave of nostalgia and had become an unexpected hit. After touring for six months, *Sugar Babies* landed at the Mark Hellinger Theater on Broadway in October 1979 and was playing to sold-out audiences and rave reviews. Rooney's comeback surpassed anything that Hollywood, or Andy Hardy for that matter, could ever have dreamed up.

The last hurrah: Joey spent four weeks on Broadway in the winter of 1981, filling in for Mickey Rooney in Sugar Babies *with Ann Miller. (Photo by Ken Howard)*

But Rooney wanted to take some time off from *Sugar Babies* to make a movie called *Leave Them Laughing*. Rooney had been in Chicago several years before, during the time that Joey and Larry were co-starring in *Mind with the Dirty Man*. Rooney had caught a performance of the show and had tucked it away for future reference. Coincidentally, Joey had actually been approached by *Sugar Babies* co-producer Harry Rigby about co-starring in the show with Rooney and Miller.

"I was tempted by the offer, but I didn't think I could stand doing the same thing for a year or two, so I turned it down," he said.

But when Rooney's movie offer came in, he called Joey and asked him to pinch-hit for him in *Sugar Babies*. It would be a four-week run, but it was Broadway. Joey was sixty-three. When would he ever get this chance again?

"I didn't think it would work," Joey said. "But I decided to at least see the show. Afterwards, I told him, 'It's crazy.' When they told me I'd have only ten days of rehearsal, I said, 'It's crazier.'

"Finally I said to myself, 'What the hell, what's the worst that can happen to you? It'll be fun.' So I said OK, and Ernie Flatt, the director and choreographer, worked with me, teaching me a few steps." One of Joey's co-stars was Maxie Furman. Forty years earlier, Furman had played on the same bill as The Bishop Brothers.

Joey made his Broadway debut on January 31, 1981, to generally positive reviews.

"Nothing demonstrates Rooney's inspired mastery more than those parts of *Sugar Babies* that have been kept more or less intact for Bishop," wrote *Philadelphia Inquirer* critic William B. Collins.

"Rooney in drag reminded you of Sophie Tucker in distress. Bishop is more in the style of *South Pacific*'s Luther Billis, with balloons instead of coconuts. Bishop . . . remembers a thing or two about the lost art of very low comedy. He knows the uses of the slow take and the fast riposte."

It was a fitting way for Joey to close out his career. The four weeks in *Sugar Babies* would be his last big hurrah, although he continued to play Vegas and Atlantic City through the mid-to-late 1980s. Joey hosted a live game show from the Palace Theater at the Claridge Hotel & Casino, wowing the bus-tour crowd and trying to help young comedians get some experience. He made some sporadic TV appearances, including a 1985 guest shot opposite Angela Lansbury in *Murder, She Wrote*. In 1986, he dropped by *Donahue* to defend Frank Sinatra after the publication of Kitty Kelley's scandalous *His Way: The Unauthorized Biography of Frank Sinatra*. "I thought Frank was gay," he joked about Sinatra's alleged dalliances. *Donahue* host Phil Donahue had an in with Joey; his wife, Marlo Thomas, had starred in the first, ill-fated season of *The Joey Bishop Show*, when Joey had reduced her to tears. Now she was an A-list celebrity married to the country's most popular daytime talk show host.

Joey talked about launching a greeting-card line, in which someone would open up a card and be greeted by a celebrity voice. It was a good idea that never materialized. Director Martin Scorsese briefly considered Joey for the role of kidnapped talk-show host Jerry Langford in *The King of Comedy*, a role that eventually went to Jerry Lewis. Joey popped up as the ghost of Alan Alda's father in the 1990 movie *Betsy's Wedding* and, in 1996, made a cameo appearance as "Mr. Gottlieb" in Larry's directorial debut, *Mad Dog Time* (starring Larry's high school buddy Richard Dreyfuss).

In between, Joey had a brief bout with skin cancer, probably accelerated by all the time he spent out in the sun at Newport Beach. His old pal, Dr. Giuffre, snipped a lesion off of Joey's nose and pronounced his patient cured.

The old Rat Pack days were now a distant memory. Peter had died a miserable, lonely death in 1984, and Sammy had checked out in 1990 after a brave battle with throat cancer. Dean, who never recovered from the death of Dino Jr. in 1987, passed away on Christmas Day 1995, a shell of his former self.

For Frank, it was a slower deterioration. His public appearances became more infrequent and he began to lose his train of thought, sometimes forgetting the words to his own classics. In 1994, Frank was honored with an honorary Grammy Award by the recording industry. He delivered a rambling, almost incoherent speech and was literally cut off in mid-sentence. Shortly thereafter he slipped out of sight, rarely appearing in public anymore.

Joey now spent his days watching a lot of television (*Wheel of Fortune* and *Jeopardy!* were favorites) and doing crossword puzzles, a hobby he had always enjoyed. In 1998, Sylvia was diagnosed with lung cancer, and Joey hired a nurse to help out around the house while he tended to his wife of fifty-seven years, running errands and making sure she was comfortable.

And then, suddenly, it was like 1960 all over again.

It started with Sinatra's death in May 1998. The huge outpouring of national grief that followed eventually evolved into a wave of Rat Pack nostalgia. Joey, now eighty and wizened, with a sunken face and white hair, was photographed at Sinatra's Hollywood funeral.

He was the last surviving member of The Rat Pack and, suddenly, those swingin' days and everything they symbolized (Kennedy-era womanizing, drinking, political incorrectness) was chic again. Kids

The last Rat Packer: Joey, 80, poses for the press after Frank Sinatra's death in May 1998. (Courtesy Getty Archives)

in their twenties, born too late to experience the Rat Pack mystique of cool the first time around, were now drinking cocktails and dressing like Frank and the guys. Independent movie houses were re-running *Ocean's 11*, and there was even talk in Hollywood of remaking the movie with an all-star cast.

Martin Scorsese talked of turning Nick Tosches' biography of Dean into a movie. Scorsese's dream cast included Tom Hanks as Dean and John Travolta as Frank (nobody suggested anyone for Joey). Two books on The Rat Pack were published in quick succession, and HBO announced that its movie, *The Rat Pack*, would air later that summer with stars Ray Liotta as Frank, Joe Mantegna as Dean, and club comic Bobby Slayton (dubbed "The Pit Bull of Comedy") as Joey. Joey sent Slayton an autographed picture with the inscription: "Please become a big star so one day I can play you." The good feelings didn't last long; Joey later complained that Slayton "ambushed" him by calling him at home, without any advance notice, while Slayton was guesting on a morning radio show.

Even Joey's old stomping grounds cashed in on The Rat Pack renaissance. Former teen idol David Cassidy, who had starred in *The Partridge Family*, mounted a stage show, first at The Desert Inn and later at The Sahara Hotel. The show, called *The Rat Pack Is Back*, was based on a fictitious 1961 Copa Room show celebrating Sinatra's forty-sixth birthday. A rotating roster of actors portrayed Frank, Dean, Sammy, Peter, and Joey.

Joey, who had been out of the spotlight for so many years, now found himself the center of attention once again as the last remnant of a bygone era. After Sinatra died, reporters flocked to Newport Beach, as Joey held court in his upstairs trophy room reminiscing about Frank, Dean, Sammy, and Peter. Joey said he had last seen Frank about eighteen months before, when they had dinner together.

"Am I happy he's dead? No," Joey said. "Am I happy he's not suffering anymore? Yes . . . You know the man is ill if he's not performing anymore.

"I tried to only call him when I had something I thought would cheer him up," Joey said. "The Rat Pack was all about fun, and illness isn't fun . . . I think he's in heaven now, and they're happy he's singin' again."

Joey told *New York Post* columnist Steve Dunleavy about a dream he'd had the night Sinatra died.

"It was the strangest thing I have ever experienced," Joey said, telling Dunleavy that he had fallen asleep in front of his TV set that night.

"Now I'm actually dreaming that I hear on TV that Frank had passed away. Now I'm saying to myself in this dream that this isn't so. That this is some kind of a hoax.

"So in my dream, I get dressed and I drive from my home at the beach to Frank's house in Beverly Hills. In my mind, I have to come face-to-face with him to prove to myself that it's true—he hasn't passed away.

"I knock on the door, and there's Frank standing there very much alive. I yell at him, 'What kind of joke is this?' Frank laughs and we go inside and start to kibitz about old times. I tell him I didn't believe the story and I remind him of the time he almost drowned in Hawaii and proved he was indestructible. He got caught in the tide and almost died. A young actor called Brad Dexter saved him.

"So, I say to Frank: 'You forgot who you were. You could have walked across the water. Frank breaks up. Then, at 7:30 the next morning, I get up to feed the cat and I hear the news that he had actually passed away. In your mind, guys like Frank never die. I went cold remembering my dream."

Suddenly, Joey was everywhere. He was the subject of a three-page feature in *TV Guide* (snapping at the writer, "I don't understand the questions that sometimes you people ask"). He was in *People* magazine, dressed in a yellow sweater and wearing a pair of boxing gloves. The magazine called him "prickly."

He materialized on CNN's *Larry King Live*, appearing with Wayne Newton, Vic Damone, Shirley Jones, George Schlatter, and Eartha Kitt to chat with host Larry King about Sinatra and his legacy ("Frank Sinatra, on my son's Bar Mitzvah in 1960, sent him a huge bond," Joey said. "This is 1998 and my son, God bless him, still has not cashed the bond. He worships Sinatra.") Joey also corrected Newton about the proper geographical location of The Latin Casino. "Is this about Frank or a geography lesson?" Schlatter shot back. Damone recalled singing at Larry's Bar Mitzvah. King seemed flustered by Joey's interruptions.

Even venerable *Time* magazine had a full-page story about Joey headlined "And Then There Was One: Joey Bishop, the sole surviving Rat Packer, fights a losing battle against myth." Joey, "good and crotchety" (writer Bruce Handy's words) used the article to lash out at the sudden Rat Pack nostalgia. "Could it be anything else but money? I don't understand this searching for things that weren't there. It's like a hunger," he said. "Everything you're hearing now is hearsay. Let me give you an example. Are we remembered as being drunks and chasing broads? I never saw Frank, Dean, Sammy, or Peter drunk during performances. That was only a gag! And do you believe these guys had to chase broads? They had to chase 'em away!"

Later that summer, retro cable network TV Land added *The Joey Bishop Show* to its lineup of sitcoms from the 1950s and 1960s. Joey directed his anger at TV Land executives who, he felt, weren't promoting the show properly. When HBO's *The Rat Pack* premiered soon thereafter, he was asked if the movie would be any good.

"How can they take what was successful about the Rat Pack, which was the spontaneity, and put that on film?" he told *People* magazine. "[The HBO movie] is only for money, my friend. What you are hearing and seeing now about the Rat Pack is hearsay. I have been married fifty-seven years. I never had a drink of liquor in my life except for wine at Passover services. I never saw Frank drunk. I never saw Dean drunk. I never saw Sammy drunk."

In September 1999, Sylvia lost her battle against lung cancer. Joey was crushed. He and Larry, respecting her final wishes, scattered Sylvia's ashes in the ocean and then waited nearly a month before informing the rest of the world of her passing. Joey gave an "exclusive" story about Sylvia's death to a supermarket tabloid.

In December 2001, Warner Bros. released its remake of *Ocean's 11*, directed by Oscar winner Steven Soderbergh and starring George Clooney as Danny Ocean (Sinatra's role in the original movie) and a host of A-list co-stars including Brad Pitt, Julia Roberts, and Don Cheadle. The movie re-ignited an interest in the original Rat Pack and grossed $30 million in its opening weekend. Original cast members Henry Silva and Angie Dickinson were invited to join the fun for a few days and were featured briefly in the movie in a ringside fight scene in Vegas. Joey took a pass. That was a movie from another time, another place.

"Give me a break. There will only ever be one Rat Pack. It's a joke," Joey told the press. "All they are doing in the remake is a cheap impersonation of the original Rat Pack. People knew about Frank and his broads and Dean and his drinking. They knew that we partied together. With the new version, you've got five or six people who never had any association with each other off screen."

It could never be 1960 again.

Okay, so I borrowed the title of this book from Joey Bishop, who, in his self-deprecating way, always said he would call his own story "I Was a Mouse in the Rat Pack." It's a standing joke he still pulls out whenever someone asks him to "tell all" about those halcyon days with Frank, Dean, Sammy, and Peter.

Still, it's a great title, and since Joey hasn't yet written his book, I've taken the liberty of using his "Mouse in the Rat Pack" analogy for this biography of a man who was anything *but* a mouse in the annals of show-biz lore.

In his prime, which encompassed roughly ten years (1959 to 1969), Joey Bishop was one of the country's best-known comedians. He was big with a capital B. Think Jerry Seinfeld in a yellow cardigan and close-cropped hair and you'll have some idea of Joey's popularity during those days.

In the early 1960s, Joey ran with Sinatra's Rat Pack, emceed JFK's inaugural, headlined in Vegas, Miami, and elsewhere, and was even interviewed on *Person to Person*.

And that's just the tip of the iceberg. Joey also co-starred in two Rat Pack movies (most memorably in *Ocean's 11*), frequently guest-hosted for Johnny Carson on the *Tonight Show*, and even forged his own popular catchphrase, "Son of a gun!" And then there was his sitcom, *The Joey Bishop Show*, which ran for four seasons at a time when there were only three networks—and a TV show was A TV SHOW, thank you very much. Cable? That was twenty years away.

People of a certain age might dust off their memory banks and recall the "Joey Joey Joey!" jingle that opened *The Joey Bishop Show*, theme music courtesy of Sinatra songwriters Jimmy Van Heusen and Sammy Cahn, to add a bit of Rat Pack panache. On any given week, celebrities like Milton Berle, Jack Benny, Andy Williams, Oscar Levant, or Rocky Marciano were likely to turn up on *The Joey Bishop Show*. Several years later, some of those same celebrities visited Joey on his ABC talk show, also called *The Joey Bishop Show*. Joey was going to topple Carson with his late-night talk show and a young sidekick named Regis Philbin. It didn't work out, of course—nobody *ever* beat Carson. Still, *The Joey Bishop Show* had a pretty good two-and-a-half year run. And it introduced Regis Philbin to America long before his association with Kathie Lee Gifford, Kelly Ripa, and *Who Wants to Be a Millionaire*. Regis has done pretty well for himself ever since and has always acknowledged Joey's role in jump-starting his career (and landing Regis his wife, Joy, who worked as Joey's secretary).

I first met Joey Bishop over the phone in the summer of 1996, when I interviewed him for *The New York Post*. At the time, I was writing a weekly Sunday feature for our television section called "The Bureau of Missing TV Persons," and I thought it would be fun to track Joey down and see what he was up to. I knew the bare outlines of Joey's career, the requisite Rat Pack stories, and the fact that he hosted a talk show with Regis Philbin. But I had always been intrigued that a comedian so prominent in the 1960s now engendered this typical response: "Whatever happened to *him*?"

I called a friend of mine in Los Angeles, Bonnie Fleming, the daughter of veteran publicist Warren Cowan (who had counted Frank, Dean, and Sammy among his many storied clients). She, in turn, put me in touch with TV writer Harry Crane, one of Joey's oldest friends, who gave me Joey's home phone number.

(Sadly, Harry has since passed away. When I interviewed Sam Denoff for this book, he told me a very funny story involving Joey and Harry. Harry, a diabetic, once felt himself growing lightheaded and staggered into Nate & Al's deli in L.A., asking the manager for an orange so he could raise his blood sugar. He then collapsed and had to be taken, by ambulance, to the hospital. Joey called Harry;

he wanted to come visit him in the hospital and needed directions. "You want to know how to get to the hospital?" said Harry. "Go to Nate & Al's and ask for an orange!")

During our first phone conversation, which probably lasted for twenty minutes or so, I found Joey to be delightful and eager to talk. He told me about his first time working with Frank Sinatra, at Bill Miller's Riviera in Fort Lee, New Jersey, and how he enjoyed doing crossword puzzles and watching *Wheel of Fortune*. He was proud of the record he had set guest-hosting the *Tonight Show* for Johnny Carson and asked me to send him the article once it was published.

Shortly thereafter, I called Joey back. He obviously was chock-full of great stories and was the only member of the Rat Pack whose own story had never been told in book form. What would he think about me writing his biography, or about the two of us collaborating on his memoirs? He told me he had been approached numerous times before to tell his story and had been offered a lot of money to do so. But he had always refused. After all, he didn't want to be perceived as boasting of his accomplishments. All publishers wanted these days was "dirt," he said, and he wasn't about to dish any gossip about himself or anyone else—particularly Frank Sinatra.

He talked bitterly about those who had written about him, becoming particularly incensed about a certain magazine writer whose caption of a snapshot of The Rat Pack had (according to Joey) said, "Why is Joey Bishop in this photo?"

That initial phone conversation led to a relationship that would play itself out for the next several years. Joey and I continued to talk over the phone every now and then; sometimes I called him, sometimes he called me. No matter how the conversation went, I always hung up feeling like I had just talked to a living legend. I was amazed that Joey was so accessible (he answered his own phone) and that he would take the time to spend hours chatting with me. It wasn't always pleasant; Joey could be sharp, cutting, and abruptly sarcastic. He could get nasty if I didn't laugh at a joke and, if I did laugh, would quiz me as to why I thought it was funny. He could be downright prickly one minute, charming and warm the next. He believed in "honesty," he said often, and he didn't hold anything back.

Our conversations inevitably got around to the book idea, and Joey waffled. He wanted to collaborate with me, but would then dismiss the idea outright. On the one hand, he seemed eager to claim his place in show-biz history as a vital member of The Rat Pack and not just "the Ringo, along for the ride," as one wag described him. After all, he held an important position in Frank Sinatra's world. Not many people could say that. On the other hand, he didn't want to be seen as tooting his own horn. People would think he was simply capitalizing on the sudden wave of interest in The Rat Pack.

When my biography of Art Carney was published, I asked Joey to write a blurb for the paperback version. He graciously agreed and put a great deal of thought into what he wanted to say. I was thrilled.

Finally, the time came for us to meet face-to-face. In January 1999, I was in Pasadena, California, on assignment for *The New York Post*, when I called Joey and asked if I could swing by the next day. He said it wouldn't be a problem.

He greeted me at the door of his Newport Beach home in a brown, crushed-velvet sweatsuit. He was wearing slippers (no socks), and he looked exactly as he had months before—gaunt and wizened—when the world's media had descended upon him after Sinatra died, looking for quotes from the last surviving Rat Packer.

We made small talk for a while in his sunken living room, which was neat and tidy. His wife, Sylvia, who was ill and would die eight months later, poked her head in briefly to say hello. Then we headed upstairs to Joey's trophy room, the walls of which were lined with plaques, photos, and other memorabilia recounting his sixty-plus years in show business.

But our conversation, which had been pleasant (if a little stilted) downstairs, became downright hairy once we got up to the trophy room. While I perused a photo of Joey and Prince Phillip hanging on the wall, Joey suddenly barked at me. I wasn't paying attention to what he was saying. How could I be paying attention to him if I was focused on that photograph? Gazing out of the picture window,

I asked him if he kept his boat moored in the water just outside. "What kind of question is that?" he snapped. "Where else would I keep it?" If I didn't laugh in the appropriate places, Joey was offended; if I didn't seem sympathetic, he was offended. I nodded my head while he was talking—the way most people do to acknowledge someone—and he accused me of not listening to him ("Why are you nodding your head like that?").

"I liked you better over the phone," he said to me at one point, staring at me to gauge my reaction. He asked me several times if he was offending me ("I believe in being honest," he repeated). He was, but I lied and said no.

Gradually, his demeanor softened. Maybe the trophy-room volleys were a hazing of sorts, Joey's way of seeing if I could withstand his verbal assaults. We went downstairs to the kitchen, where Joey ate his lunch (a hard-boiled egg and a chocolate milkshake). He told me I had "a beautiful head of hair" and was disappointed that I didn't want anything to eat. We went back into the living room, where Joey proudly showed me a book from the 1960s in which comedians (him included) talked about the essence of their comedy. He began to open up about The Rat Pack and, to my astonishment, began performing part of their act, feeding me lines (I was Dean and Sammy) while he delivered the old jokes. It was surreal—Joey, eighty-one and in his brown velvet sweatsuit, transporting himself back to the Copa Room in The Sands. For a brief moment, it was 1960 again.

We talked, briefly, about resuscitating the book idea, and then I was out the door. The two hours I had spent with Joey seemed like an eternity.

Joey is eighty-four now, and his performing days are long behind him. In late January 2001, I wrote him a letter telling him that I was writing this book. In the letter, I said that I understood if he didn't want to participate in my book, but that I would welcome his input at any time. A week later, Joey called me at *The New York Post*. "What do *you* know about *me?*" he asked pointedly. I told him that, as a biographer, I hoped to learn more about his life and career by interviewing people like Garry Marshall. Joey had brought Marshall out to California (at his own expense) in the early 1960s to write for *The Joey Bishop Show*. Marshall, like Regis Philbin, was always quick to credit Joey with giving him his first big break.

"Garry Marshall is an asshole," Joey retorted. Why? Because Marshall, in his autobiography, had written that part of Joey's act—in which he threw a hat into the air, let it fall and proclaimed, "For what they're paying me, I don't catch hats"—didn't work once he made it big in Vegas "because now he was being paid well." (For the record, Marshall declined to be interviewed for this book.)

In writing about Joey's life and career, and in speaking to people who knew him in different capacities (writers, friends, co-stars), I came away with the sense of a man who knew what he wanted, worked for years to achieve it, and then let it go—much too quickly. Joey was only fifty-one when *The Joey Bishop Show* was cancelled in 1969 but, for all intents and purposes, it signaled the end of his career after a remarkable ten years on top.

Some have suggested to me that Joey never got over the failure of *The Joey Bishop Show* on such a national stage as nightly network television. And it certainly is curious that a man who had worked so hard to reach the pinnacle of show-biz—who slaved for over twenty years in nightclubs and didn't really "make it" until he was over forty—would retreat because of a failed TV show. Heck, that's a veritable badge of honor in Hollywood.

Maybe Joey, like The Beatles, was simply of his time—a product of the 1960s whose sensibilities fit snugly into that decade. Maybe he was savvy enough to realize that and decided to throw in the towel while he was ahead. Maybe he felt that he had nothing left to prove.

The question I was most often asked while writing this book was, "Why Joey Bishop?" Well, here's why: I hope that people reading this book will come away with a sense of just how big Joey was in his heyday, of how pervasive he was in the media (TV, newspapers, magazines, movies) of the 1960s. Of how, once upon a time, Joey Bishop was one of this country's biggest and most successful comedians. Of how Joey Bishop was a vital part of American pop culture.

When I began my research, I was amazed at the thickness of Joey's "clip file" at *The New York Post*. The file, a collection of yellowed magazine and newspaper clippings, was divided into two overstuffed envelopes covering roughly thirty years. That, in itself, told me all I needed to know regarding the impact Joey Bishop had on the world of entertainment.

During the writing of this book, many people told me, with not a little condescension, that Joey was simply "an appendage" of the Rat Pack. Joey was a "peripheral" member, they said, who didn't contribute much beyond playing traffic cop for the stage antics of Frank, Dean, Sammy, and Peter.

I hope that I have proven them wrong.

A Complete Episode Guide to

THE JOEY BISHOP SHOW

Author's Note: The following is an episode-by-episode guide to Joey's sitcom, *The Joey Bishop Show*, which ran on NBC from September 1961 to September 1964 and for one season on CBS (from September 1964 to September 1965). Joey hated that first season of *The Joey Bishop Show* and has never allowed those episodes to be repeated. Detailed information on those episodes, other than their titles and airdates (in parentheses), is unavailable. Otherwise, I have provided as much detail as I could find for the other seasons (cast, writers, producer, etc.).

THE FIRST SEASON: WEDNESDAYS AT 8:30 P.M. ON NBC

Pilot: "Everything Happens To Me." Aired on *Make Room for Daddy* on March 27, 1961.

"On the Spot" (9/21/61)

"Joey Meets Jack Paar" (9/27/61)

"A Windfall for Mom" (10/4/61)

"This Is Your Life" (10/11/61)

"The Contest Winner" (10/18/61)

"The Bachelor" (10/25/61)

"Help Wanted" (10/29/61)

Joey played a meek public-relations man in the first season of The Joey Bishop Show. *This shot is from "The Bachelor," the show's debut episode (September 20, 1961) on NBC.*

"Five Brides for Joey" (11/1/61)

"Back in Your Own Backyard" (11/8/61)

"Charity Begins at Home" (11/15/61)

"Ring-A-Ding-Ding" (11/22/61)

"Ham in the Family" (12/6/61)

"Follow that Mink" (12/13/61)

"Barney, the Bloodhound" (12/27/61)

"Taming of the Brat" (1/3/62)

"Home Sweet Home"(1/10/62)

"A Letter from Stella" (1/17/62)

"Jury Duty" (1/24/62)

"The Income Tax Caper" (1/31/62)

"Double Exposure" (2/7/62)

"A Man's Best Friend" (2/14/62)

"Very Warm for Christmas" (2/21/62)

"The Big Date" (2/28/62)

"Joey Hires a Maid" (3/7/62)

"That's Showbiz" (3/14/62)

"A Young Man's Fancy" (3/21/62)

"Surprise, Surprise" (3/28/62)

"Must the Show Go On?" (4/11/62)

"Once a Bachelor" (4/18/62)

"Route 78" (4/25/62)

"A Show of His Own" (5/2/62)

"The Image" (5/9/62)

THE SECOND SEASON: SATURDAYS AT 8:30 P.M. ON NBC

"The Honeymoon" (9/15/62)

Synopsis: On the night he's supposed to marry Ellie, Joey is asked to fill in for Danny Thomas at a nightclub in Las Vegas. With the nuptials looming, Joey turns down the request—only to learn a few hours after the marriage that his manager has accepted the engagement beginning that night.

Written by: Iz Elinson and Fred S. Fox

Directed by: James V. Kern

Produced by: Marvin Marx

Cast: Joey Bishop, Abby Dalton, Guy Marks, Joe Besser

"Penguin's Three" (9/22/62)

Synopsis: Joey refuses to be in the show at Jillson's lodge, The Penguins. So Jillson annoys and harasses Joey until he says that he will be in the show.

Written by: Fred Freeman and Garry Marshall

Directed by: James V. Kern

Produced by: Marvin Marx

Cast: Joey Bishop, Abby Dalton, Guy Marks, Joe Besser, Mary Treen

"Three's a Crowd" (9/29/62)

Synopsis: Ellie is getting fed up with Freddy, who keeps barging in on her dinners with Joey. When Freddy crashes the couple's three-month wedding anniversary, Ellie tells Joey to get rid of him.

Written by: Harry Crane and Stan Dreben

Directed by: James V. Kern

Produced by: Marvin Marx

Cast: Joey Bishop, Abby Dalton, Guy Marks, Joe Besser

"Door to Door Salesman" (10/6/62)

Synopsis: Joey tries to cure Ellie of her irresistible desire to buy things she doesn't need from every pitchman with a hard-luck story.

Written by: Fred S. Fox and Iz Elinson

Directed by: James V. Kern

Produced by: Marvin Marx

Cast: Joey Bishop, Abby Dalton, Fuzzy Knight (as salesman), Buddy Lewis (as salesman)

"Joey's Replacement" (10/13/62)

Synopsis: Joey is reluctant to take a sorely needed vacation when the sponsor of his TV show picks an unknown comic to fill in.

Written by: Harry Crane and Stan Dreben

Directed by: James V. Kern

Produced by: Marvin Marx

Cast: Joey Bishop, Abby Dalton, Guy Marks, Joe Besser, Corbett Monica (as Johnny Edwards), Joey Faye (as waiter), Paul Maxey (as Mr. Hendricks), Maxine Semon (as Mrs. Jillson)

"The Fashion Show" (10/20/62)

Synopsis: Joey and Freddy arrive at Joey's apartment unexpectedly to find Ellie dressed to the nines. Joey gets even more suspicious when he learns that Ellie is meeting a man named Roger, whom she tries to pass off as the plumber.

Written by: Harry Crane and Stan Dreben

Directed by: James V. Kern

Produced by: Marvin Marx

Cast: Joey Bishop, Abby Dalton, Guy Marks, Joe Besser, Patrick Waltz (as Roger), Eleanor Audley (as fashion announcer), Maxine Semon (as Mrs. Jillson)

"The Break-Up" (10/27/62)

Synopsis: Freddy gets so irritated at Joey's mandolin playing that the two men decide to end their lifelong friendship. But when Freddy tries for a new job he needs Joey's recommendation. Joey writes a horrible recommendation for Freddy, who resolves his differences with his boss and remains as Joey's manager.

Written by: Harry Crane and Stan Dreben

Directed by: James V. Kean

Produced by: Marvin Marx

Cast: Joey Bishop, Abby Dalton, Guy Marks

"A Woman's Place" (11/3/62)

Synopsis: Joey's gags about women politicians on his TV show spurs Ellie to announce that she's running for the Assembly. Freddy and Joey think they'll embarrass Ellie and fix her wagon by letting her go on TV to discuss American history. But Ellie knows more than they think, and makes a fool out of Joey.

Written by: Fred S. Fox and Iz Elinson

Directed by: James V. Kern

Produced by: Marvin Marx

Cast: Joey Bishop, Abby Dalton, Guy Marks, Mary Treen, Eleanor Audley, Shirley Mitchell, Ellie Kent, Myrna Ross, Joanne Barr and Susan Kelly as Clubwomen

"Baby, It's Cold Inside" (11/10/62)

Synopsis: Ellie and Joey reluctantly become hosts to an Eskimo dog that Jillson won in a jingle contest. But the dog must have the apartment freezing, and Joey complains all the time. He and Ellie stay in Jillson's basement apartment with all types of animals.

Written by: Harry Crane and Stan Dreben

Directed by: James V. Kern

Produced by: Marvin Marx

Cast: Joey Bishop, Abby Dalton, Joe Besser

"Joey Takes a Physical" (11/17/62)

Synopsis: Ellie, who's weary of hearing Joey's excuses for neglecting to take his regular medical checkup, cooks up an elaborate scheme to make him think he's sick. When the scheme fails, Freddy brings in old vaudeville star, Max Collins, to hypnotize Joey.

Written by: Iz Elinson and Fred S. Fox

Directed by: James V. Kern

Produced by: Marvin Marx

Cast: Joey Bishop, Abby Dalton, Guy Marks, Joe Besser, Benny Rubin (as Max Collins)

"Deep in the Heart of Texas" (11/24/62)

Synopsis: Joey feels that Ellie is homesick for Texas, so he decides to take her to Texas. But Joey can't leave his show, so Freddy decides to bring Texas to Ellie.

Written by: Harry Crane and Stan Dreben

Directed by: James V. Kern

Produced by: Marvin Marx

Cast: Joey Bishop, Abby Dalton, Guy Marks, The Frontiersman and Joanie

"The Honeymoon Is Over" (12/1/62)

Synopsis: Joey announces that he plans an evening out with the boys, and Ellie gets the idea that "the wolf wants to howl again." The more Ellie thinks about Joey's night out, the angrier she gets—and plots a retaliatory strike.

Written by: Iz Elinson and Fred S. Fox

Directed by: James V. Kern

Produced by: Marvin Marx

Cast: Joey Bishop, Abby Dalton, Guy Marks, Joe Besser, Mary Treen

"Chance of a Lifetime" (12/8/62)

Synopsis: Seeking a good investment opportunity for Joey, Freddy finds a boxer, Willy, who looks like he will be a champ—even though he has never fought a professional bout. Joey ends up wasting money on Willie, who never amounts to anything.

Written by: Harry Crane and Stan Dreben

Directed by: James V. Kern

Cast: Joey Bishop, Abby Dalton, Guy Marks, Joe Besser, Herbie Faye (as Charlie), Peter Lupus (as Willie), Mel Bishop (as man), Maxine Semon (as Mrs. Jillson)

"Joey's Lucky Cufflinks" (12/15/62)

Synopsis: Joey is about to perform at an important dinner attended by the governor when he discovers he can't find his lucky cufflinks—and refuses to go on without them.

Written by: Fred S. Fox and Iz Elinson

Story by: Fred Freeman and Garry Marshall

Directed by: James V. Kern

Cast: Joey Bishop, Abby Dalton, Guy Marks, Joe Besser, Jane Dulo (as Mrs. Tribly), Muriel Landers (as Mrs. Cosgrove)

"Wife versus Secretary" (12/22/62)

Synopsis: Ellie gets jealous when Joey misses five straight meals to work overtime with his new secretary, Cindy.

Written by: Iz Elinson and Fred S. Fox

Directed by: James V. Kern

Produced by: Marvin Marx

Cast: Joey Bishop, Abby Dalton, Guy Marks, Joe Besser, Carol Byron (as Cindy)

"Kiss and Make Up" (12/29/62)

Synopsis: Ellie's friend Doris convinces Ellie that she needs a make-up kiss from Joey since they've never had a fight. Ellie tries to provoke Joey into a fight, but he's not biting—until Freddy gets involved.

Written by: Iz Elinson and Fred S. Fox

Directed by: James V. Kern

Cast: Joey Bishop, Abby Dalton, Guy Marks, Joe Besser, Christine Nelson (as Doris), Maxine Semon (as Mrs. Jillson)

"Double Time" (1/5/63)

Synopsis: Joey Bishop plays dual roles as Joey Barnes and nearsighted convict Louie. After Joey entertains inmates at a nearby prison, Louie knocks Joey unconscious and changes clothes with him. Later, at Joey's apartment, Louie even fools Ellie. Joey, meanwhile, is thrown into Louie's cell and tries to convince his cellmate that the whole thing has been a terrible mistake.

Cast: Joey Bishop, Abby Dalton, Guy Marks, Joe Besser, Addison Richards (as warden), Mel Bishop (as Melina), Johnny Silver (as Sytes), Maxine Semon (as Mrs. Jillson), Sheldon Leonard (as cellmate)

"Jillson and the Cinnamon Buns" (1/12/63)

Synopsis: Jillson is a guest on Joey's talk show, and Joey tells his audience how Jillson is on a diet. Mrs. Jillson calls everyone in the apartment building and tells them that Jillson is on a diet—and not to give him any cinnamon buns. Desperate for the sweet treats, Jillson goes and buys every cinnamon bun that he can find—and hides them in every apartment.

Written by: Fred S. Fox and Iz Elinson

Directed by: James V. Kern

Cast: Joey Bishop, Abby Dalton, Guy Marks, Joe Besser, Mary Treen

"Freddy Goes Highbrow" (1/19/63)

Synopsis: Freddy fakes a British accent and mannerisms to impress his society girlfriend.

Cast: Joey Bishop, Abby Dalton, Guy Marks, Joe Besser, Mary Treen

"Joey Leaves Ellie" (1/26/63)

Synopsis: Joey has judo expert Gloria Williams on his TV show, and his behavior with her upsets Ellie, who throws Joey out of the house.

Written by: Ray Singer and Dick Chevillat

Directed by: James V. Kern

Cast: Joey Bishop, Abby Dalton, Corbett Monica (as Larry), Joe Besser, Joi Lansing (as Gloria Williams), Mary Treen, Maxine Semon (as Mrs. Jillson)

"Ellie, the Talent Scout" (2/2/63)

Synopsis: Joey regrets his decision to let Ellie choose the talent for one of his TV shows when she holds auditions in their living room.

Written by: Fred S. Fox and Iz Elinson

Directed by: James. V Kern

Cast: Joey Bishop, Abby Dalton, Corbett Monica, Joe Besser, The Sportsmen, Henry Gibson, Marjorie Bennett

"A Crush on Joey" (2/16/63)

Synopsis: To discourage an eight-year-old girl's crush on him, Joey invites her to a rehearsal of his show and acts like a tyrant, firing members of his production staff and browbeating his performers.

Written by: Fred Freeman and Garry Marshall

Directed by: James V. Kern

Cast: Joey Bishop, Abby Dalton, Corbett Monica, Joe Besser, Milton Frome (as the director), Joanne Barr (as the script girl), Michel Petit (as Michael), Katie Sweet (as Penny), Billy Barty (as the midget), Mel Bishop (first stagehand), Maxine Semon

"Joey's Houseguest" (2/23/63)

Synopsis: Aunt Celia is on her way for a visit—much to Joey's chagrin. Now he's got to make sure the guest room stays occupied so there's no room for her.

Cast: Joey Bishop, Abby Dalton, Joe Besser, Corbett Monica

"We're Going to Have a Baby" (3/2/63)

Synopsis: Joey tells his TV audience that Ellie is expecting their first child.

Cast: Joey Bishop, Abby Dalton, Joe Besser, Corbett Monica

"The Baby Formula" (3/9/63)

Synopsis: Joey and Larry get stuck babysitting a neighbor's baby and end up turning the afternoon into a disaster.

Written by: Ray Singer and Dick Chevillat

Directed by: James V. Kern

Cast: Joey Bishop, Abby Dalton, Corbett Monica, Joe Besser, Henry Gibson (as Henry Schultz), Mary Grace Canfield (as Mrs. Bennett)

"Joey's Dramatic Debut" (3/16/63)

Synopsis: Joey tries switching from comedy to dramatic acting and gets a sore jaw for his trouble.

"Joey and the Laundry" (3/23/63)

Synopsis: Laundresses Natalie Tribly and Mildred Cosgrove are dying to get on Joey's TV show and try conning him by putting starch in his shorts. Joey tells the women they can appear on the show so they can plug their laundry, and he ends up singing and dancing with them on the air.

Written by: Iz Elinson and Fred S. Fox

Directed by: James V. Kern

Cast: Joey Bishop, Abby Dalton, Corbett Monica, Joe Besser, Jane Dulo (as Natalie), Muriel Landers (as Mildred), Maxine Semon (as Mrs. Jillson)

"The Masquerade Party" (3/30/63)

Synopsis: Joey is supposed to go to a masquerade party dressed as Robin Hood, but he changes his mind at the last minute—and decides to go in a matador's outfit, because he sees himself as slim and dashing.

Written by: Fred S. Fox and Iz Elinson

Directed by: James V. Kern

Cast: Joey Bishop, Abby Dalton, Corbett Monica, Joe Besser, Mary Treen

"Joey, the Good Samaritan" (4/6/63)

Synopsis: Laundresses Natalie Tribly and Mildred Cosgrove are back, and this time they're trying to con Joey into letting Mildred's niece, Gina, get her big break as an opera singer on Joey's TV show.

Written by: Ray Singer and Dick Chevillat

Directed by: James V. Kern

Cast: Joey Bishop, Abby Dalton, Corbett Monica, Joe Besser, Mary Treen, Jane Dulo (as Natalie), Muriel Landers (as Mildred), Betty Santora (as Gina)

"My Son, the Doctor" (4/13/63)

Synopsis: Joey informs Ellie that their child will be a boy and a doctor, while Larry wants the baby to be a lawyer and Hilda, the maid, wants the baby to be an actor. Joey, using some prenatal influence, repeats "Our son is going to be a doctor." This leads to a dream sequence with Jillson needing an operation and seven-year-old Joey Barnes Jr. (played by Joey Bishop) performing the operation.

Written by: Iz Elinson and Fred S. Fox

Directed by: James V. Kern

Cast: Joey Bishop, Abby Dalton, Corbett Monica, Joe Besser, Herbie Barris (as Dr. Flugelmayer)

"The Expectant Father's School" (4/20/63)

Synopsis: Joey graduates "validiaperatorian" of his expectant father's class and becomes a know-it-all about babies.

Written by: Garry Marshall and Fred Freeman

Directed by: James V. Kern

Cast: Joey Bishop, Abby Dalton, Corbett Monica, Joe Besser, Gordon Jones (as the delivery man)

"The Baby Nurse" (4/27/63)

Synopsis: Ellie tries to convince Joey that their maid, Hilda, would be the perfect nanny for their baby.

Cast: Joey Bishop, Abby Dalton, Joe Besser, Corbett Monica, Mary Treen

"My Buddy, My Buddy" (5/4/63)

Synopsis: Joey's pal Buddy Hackett shows up, unannounced, at Joey and Ellie's apartment and unleashes a torrent of practical jokes, including some shenanigans with a baby elephant. Joey plots his revenge with the help of a surprise celebrity guest.

Written by: Stan Dreben and Ralph Goodman

Directed by: James V. Kern

Cast: Joey Bishop, Abby Dalton, Corbett Monica, Joe Besser, Buddy Hackett, Milton Frome (as policeman), Mel Bishop (as second policeman)

"The Baby Cometh" (5/11/63)

Synopsis: Joey is so excited when Ellie tells him that "it's time" that he almost leaves for the hospital without her and then remains a nervous wreck until it's all over.

Written by: Ray Singer and Dick Chevillat

Directed by: James V. Kern

Cast: Joey Bishop, Abby Dalton, Corbett Monica, Joe Besser, Mary Treen, Frank Wilcox (as the doctor), Natalie Masters and Shirley Christian (as nurses), Miskey Manners, Lenny Kent, Buddy Lewis, Patrick Waltz and Mel Bishop (as expectant fathers)

THE THIRD SEASON: SUNDAYS AT 9:30 P.M. ON NBC

"The Baby's First Day" (9/21/63)

Synopsis: Joey brings Ellie and their new baby, Joey Jr., home from the hospital, and he becomes overly concerned about the baby. Joey insists everyone who comes near Joey Jr. must wear a mask—which leads to complications when Joey himself is suspected of being an armed bandit.

Written by: Harry Crane and John Tackaberry

Directed by: James V. Kern

Produced by: Milt Josefsberg

Cast: Joey Bishop, Abby Dalton, Corbett Monica, Joe Besser, Mary Treen, Sandra Gould (as saleswoman), William Keene (as pharmacist), Buddy Lewis (as first policeman), Anthony Lettier (as second policeman), Mack Pearson (as Lefty), Jonny Silver (as witness), Karen Norris (as witness)

"Joey Plugs the Laundry" (9/28/63)

Synopsis: Mildred Tribly and Natalie Cosgrove are back for a third time, this time conning Joey into plugging their laundromat on his show. Joey winds up being sued for slander for putting down the other laundromats, and, is then sued by Mildred and Natalie's laundry when he goes to clear his name.

Written by: Ray Singer and Dick Chevillat

Directed by: James V. Kern

Produced by: Milt Josefsberg

Cast: Joey Bishop, Abby Dalton, Joe Besser, Mary Treen, Jane Dulo (as Natalie), Muriel Landers (as Mildred), Herbert Rudley (as Mr. Hobbs), John Alvin (as Mr. Harper), Matthew David Smith (as Joey Barnes Jr.)

"Joey's Mustache" (10/5/63)

Synopsis: When Joey is sick for two weeks and doesn't shave, his barber, Frank, creates a "masterpiece"—leaving Joey with a small, neat mustache.

Cast: Joey Bishop, Abby Dalton, Joe Besser, Corbett Monica, Vito Scotti (as Frank).

"Danny Gives Joey Advice" (10/12/63)

Synopsis: Guest star Danny Thomas and Joey play their own teenage sons in a spoof of "spare the rod and spoil the child." The two comedians reminisce about their own simple childhoods, and Danny cautions Joey not to spoil his newborn son.

Written by: Iz Elinson and Fred S. Fox

Directed by: James V. Kern

Produced by: Milt Josefsberg

Cast: Joey Bishop, Corbett Monica, Joe Besser, Mary Treen, Danny Thomas, Matthew David Smith (as Joey Barnes Jr.)

"The Babysitter" (10/19/63)

Synopsis: Ellie is disappointed when she and Joey miss their big night out on the town because their babysitter cancelled—so Joey stages his own show.

Written by: Harry Crane and Ernest Chambers

Directed by: James V. Kern

Produced by: Milt Josefsberg

Cast: Joey Bishop, Abby Dalton, Joe Besser, Mary Treen, Amedee Charbot, Madeline Reed and Leslie Perkins (as bathing beauties), Tommy Ivo (as page boy), Matthew David Smith

"Joey's Lost What-Cha-Ma-Call-It" (10/26/63)

Synopsis: Joey and Ellie are notified that a valuable item has been found in the hotel room they occupied, and if they can describe this object, they get to take it home with them.

Written by: Harry Crane and Ernest Chambers

Directed by: James V. Kern

Produced by: Milt Josfesberg

Cast: Joey Bishop, Abby Dalton, Corbett Monica, Joe Besser, Mary Treen, Barbara Morrison (as woman at telephone), Robert Paget (as page boy), Sterling Holloway (as Mr. Holland), Jack Benny (as himself)

"Two Little Maids Are We" (11/1/63)

Synopsis: Ellie, Hilda, and Joey Jr. go to visit Ellie's parents back home in Texas, leaving Joey and Larry to take care of themselves.

Written by: Ray Singer and Dick Chevillat

Directed by: James V. Kern

Produced by: Milt Josefsberg

Cast: Joey Bishop, Abby Dalton, Corbett Monica, Joe Besser, Mary Treen, Vito Scotti (as supermarket manager), Charity Grace (as shopper), Nora Marlowe (as shopper), Mel Bishop (as shopper), Matthew David Smith

"Joey's Surprise for Ellie" (11/9/63)

Synopsis: Joey buys Ellie a brunette wig as an "unbirthday present," but his intentions are misconstrued when he realizes that she really likes the wig.

Written by: Stan Dreben and Ralph Goodman

Directed by: James V. Kern

Produced by: Milt Josfesberg

Cast: Joey Bishop, Abby Dalton, Corbett Monica, Joe Besser, Mary Treen, Cindy O'Hara (as camera girl), Beverly Adams (as cigarette girl), Buddy Lewis (as toastmaster), Laura Hale (as bride), Bob Dunlap (as groom)

"Vic Damone Brainwashes Joey" (11/23/63)

Synopsis: Vic Damone plays himself in this cloak-and-dagger episode in which Joey thinks both he and Vic are Soviet spies.

Teleplay by: Danny Simon and Mily Rosen

Directed by: James V. Kern

Produced by: Milt Josefsberg

Cast: Joey Bishop, Abby Dalton, Corbett Monica, Vic Damone, Barry Kelley (as the general), Mickey Manners (as Parnello), Patrick Waltz (as the waiter)

Author's note: This episode aired one day after the assassination of President John F. Kennedy

"Joey Junior's TV Debut" (11/30/63)

Synopsis: Joey has Ellie and Joey Jr. on his TV show, but Ellie is extremely nervous—while Jillson and Hilda insist they're now part of the Barnes family.

Written by: Ray Singer and Dick Chevillat

Directed by: James V. Kern

Produced by: Milt Josefsberg

Cast: Joey Bishop, Abby Dalton, Corbett Monica, Joe Besser, Mary Treen, Charles Cantor (as Charlie), Matthew David Smith

"Bobby Rydell Plugs Ellie's Song" (12/14/63)

Synopsis: Special guest Bobby Rydell sings to ease the tense situation between Joey and Ellie and is trapped into promoting an amateurish song composed by Ellie.

Written by: Harry Crane and John Tackaberry

Directed by: James V. Kern

Produced by: Milt Josefsberg

Cast: Joey Bishop, Abby Dalton, Corbett Monica, Bobby Rydell, Charles Cantor (as Mr. Cosgrove), Gene Di Novi (as piano player), Jaclyn Carmicheal, Judy Short and Ann Doucette (as pompom girls)

"The Baby's First Christmas" (12/21/63)

Synopsis: Joey and Jillson differ over who would make a better Santa for Joey Jr.'s first Christmas.

"Ellie Gives Joey First Aid" (12/28/63)

Synopsis: Ellie puts a cast on Joey arm as first aid practice and winds up cutting off the circulation in his arm.

Written by: Ralph Gooman and Stan Dreben

Directed by: James V. Kern

Produced by: Milt Josefsberg

Cast: Joey Bishop, Abby Dalton, Corbett Monica, Mary Treen, Christine Nelson (as the head nurse), Joan Stanley (as the private nurse), Maidie Norman (as Nurse Mildred), Mel Bishop (as the doctor), Hy Terman (as Sheldon)

"Jack Carter Helps Joey Propose" (1/4/64)

Synopsis: Special guest Jack Carter and his wife, Paula Stewart, reminisce about the date they had with Joey when he first proposed to Ellie.

Written by: Harry Crane and Garry Marshall

Directed by: James V. Kern

Produced by: Milt Josefsberg

Cast: Joey Bishop, Abby Dalton, Jack Carter, Paula Stewart, Lenny Kent (as the waiter), Merry Anders (as Barbara), Herkie Styles (as Herkie), Bobby Bell (as Bobby), Mel Bishop (as man in booth), Jesslyhn Fax (as woman in library)

"Joey's Hideaway Cabin" (1/25/64)

Synopsis: Joey needs a rest from the pressures of his TV show, so Ellie rents a cabin that's as remote as remote can be—in a place called Hoppawattomie Falls.

Written by: Harvey Helm and Paul Bregman

Directed by: James. V. Kern

Produced by: Milt Josefsberg

Cast: Joey Bishop, Abby Dalton, Corbett Monica, Joe Besser, Mary Treen, Don Knotts (as Deputy Sheriff Barney Fife)

"*Two Little Maids Are We*": Joey and Larry (Corbett Monica) fend for themselves when Ellie goes to visit her parents in Texas.

"Zsa Zsa Redecorates the Nursery" (2/1/64)

Synopsis: Joey's guest Zsa Zsa Gabor decides to decorate Joey Jr.'s nursery because it doesn't look very masculine. But her efforts come out horribly and Ellie hates it, causing a mini-insurrection.

Written by: Iz Elinson and Fred S. Fox

Directed by: James V. Kern

Produced by: Milt Josefsberg

Cast: Joey Bishop, Abby Dalton, Corbett Monica, Zsa Zsa Gabor, Jeanne Baird (as Susan)

"Double Play: From Foster to Joey to Durocher" (2/8/64)

Synopsis: Joey's pal, comedian Phil Foster, has never forgiven the Dodgers for moving from Brooklyn to Los Angeles, but the Dodgers still remember Phil as their number-one fan. Dodgers manager Leo Durocher gives Joey the impossible task of getting Phil to act as emcee at a testimonial dinner for the Dodgers.

Written by: Bill Persky and Sam Denoff

Directed by: James V. Kern

Produced by: Milt Josefsberg

Cast: Joey Bishop, Abby Dalton, Joe Besser, Phil Foster, Leo Durocher, Lenny Kent (as the waiter)

"Joey Insults Jack E. Leonard" (2/15/64)

Synopsis: Joey and Jack E. Leonard have a disagreement over a teddy bear that Leonard has bought for Joey Jr.

Written by: Garry Marshall and Jerry Belson

Directed by: James V. Kern

Cast: Joey Bishop, Abby Dalton, Corbett Monica, Joe Besser, Mary Treen, Jack E. Leonard, Dave Ketchem (as the floorwalker), Matthew David Smith

"Joey, the Comedian versus Larry, the Writer" (2/22/64)

Synopsis: Joey's ego is battered when his writer, Larry, gets the TV Critics Award as best comedy writer of the year—and Joey doesn't even make the top ten best comedians.

Written by: Ray Singer and Dick Chevillat

Directed by: James V. Kern

Cast: Joey Bishop, Abby Dalton, Corbett Monica, Joe Besser, Mary Treen, Robert S. Carson (as the museum guide)

"Joey and Roberta Sherwood Play a Benefit" (2/29/64)

Synopsis: Joey and Roberta Sherwood are frustrated by hiccups and feminine vanity when they try to surprise Ellie with a Mother of the Year award.

Written by: Ray Singer and Dick Chevillat

Directed by: James V. Kern

Cast: Joey Bishop, Abby Dalton, Corbett Monica, Mary Treen, Roberta Sherwood, Dawn Wells (as Marilyn), Barbara Burgess (as club president)

"Joey and Buddy Have a Luau" (3/7/64)

Synopsis: On the night Joey is supposed to entertain his sponsor, Buddy Hackett plays a cruel practical joke, getting rid of all of Joey's furniture and creating a Hawaiian luau.

Written by: Stan Dreben, Ralph Goodman and Jerry Belson

Story by: Stan Dreben and Ralph Goodman

Directed by: James V. Kern

Cast: Joey Bishop, Abby Dalton, Corbett Monica, Joe Besser, Mary Treen, Buddy Hackett, Mel Bishop (as mover), Peter Leeds (as Mr. Montgomery). Luau guests: Laura Gile, Mary Benoit, Myrna Ross, Allan Ray, Paul Power, Karl Redcoff

"Hilda Quits" (3/14/64)

Synopsis: When Joey and Ellie think Hilda is going to leave them, they suddenly realize that she is the most important person in their lives, and they decide to do anything to stop her from leaving.

"Every Dog Should Have a Boy" (3/28/64)

Synopsis: Joey casually mentions on his TV show that he plans to buy a dog for Joey Jr., and suddenly loyal viewers shower him with two-dozen dogs.

"Weekend in the Mountains" (4/4/64)

Synopsis: Guest comedians Al Fisher and Lou Marks reminisce with Joey about how comedians are made—not born—in the Catskill Mountains. The fifteenth reunion of the staff and guests of Wanapotchatushi Lodge revives memories of the days when Joey presses his weary and overworked entertainers into service "beyond the call of duty" on a rainy summer's day.

Written by: Ray Singer and Dick Chevillat

Directed by: James V. Kern

Cast: Joey Bishop, Abby Dalton, Joe Besser, Mary Treen, Al Fisher, Lou Marks, Mitlon Frome (as J. J. Gerard), Mel Bishop (as hotel guest), Irving Burns (as hotel guest)

"Joey, Jack Jones, and Genie" (4/11/64)

Synopsis: Joey has a dream in which he becomes the country's leading rock star, Joey Grasshopper, with the help of guest stars Jack Jones and Ed McMahon.

"Joey Introduces Shecky Greene" (4/18/64)

Synopsis: Shecky Greene guest stars as a butcher who traps Joey in a cooler in order to get an audition for Joey's TV show.

"Andy Williams Visits Joey" (4/25/64)

Synopsis: A battle of the sexes flares when guest stars Andy Williams and his wife, Claudine Longet, pay a call on Joey and Ellie. Aware that their wives have arranged for them to be "surprise" guest entertainers at their Ladies' Club dinner for the fifth consecutive year, Joey and Andy openly defy their wives and decide on a "sit-down" strike.

Written by: Ray Singer and Dick Chevillat

Directed by: James V. Kern

Cast: Joey Bishop, Abby Dalton, Andy Williams, Claudine Longet, Danny Thomas, Robert Goulet, Barbara Burgess (as the chairlady)

"Joey Meets Edgar Bergen" (5/9/64)

Synopsis: Ventriloquist Edgar Bergen is a guest on Joey's TV show and teaches Joey the rudiments of ventriloquism. Joey decides to play a practical joke on Ellie by making her think Joey Jr. can talk.

Written by: Harry Crane and John Trackaberry

Directed by: James V. Kern

Produced by: Milt Josefsberg

Cast: Joey Bishop, Abby Dalton, Corbett Monica, Mary Treen, Edgar Bergen, Matthew David Smith

"Joey and Milton and Baby Makes Three" (5/23/64)

Synopsis: Joey is fighting a losing battle trying to get Milton Berle into the studio to rehearse for a guest appearance on Joey's TV show. It turns out Uncle Miltie is too busy supervising Joey Jr.'s homecoming from the hospital.

Written by: Fred S. Fox and Iz Elinson

Directed by: James V. Kern

Produced by: Milt Josefsberg

Cast: Joey Bishop, Corbett Monica, Joe Besser, Mary Treen, Milton Berle

"Joey and The Andrew Sisters" (5/30/64)

Synopsis: The Andrews Sisters (Patty, Maxine, and LaVerne) are going to sing on Joey's TV show, but Joey wants to sing along with them. They tell Joey he can't sing, hurting his feelings.

Written by: Harry Crane and Garry Marshall

Directed by: James V. Kern

Produced by: Milt Josefsberg

Cast: Joey Bishop, Corbett Monica, The Andrews Sisters

"Joey and The Los Angeles Dodgers" (9/5/64)

Synopsis: Desperate for a guest star for his talk show after an ill Tony Bennett bows out, Joey lines up six members of the Los Angeles Dodgers, and together they perform a song, dance, and comedy act.

Written by: Garry Marshall and Jerry Belson

Cast: Joey Bishop, Corbett Monica, Abby Dalton, Mary Treen, Joe Besser

THE FOURTH SEASON: TUESDAYS AT 8 P.M. ON CBS

"Joey Goes to CBS" (9/27/64)

Synopsis: Joey has just moved into a new penthouse apartment when he learns his television show has been canceled by NBC. So he goes to CBS, and his show gets picked up.

Written by: Jerry Belson and Garry Marshall

Directed by: Jerry Paris

Produced by: Charles Stewart

Cast: Joey Bishop, Abby Dalton, Corbett Monica, Joe Besser, Mary Treen, Lenny Kent (as Max), Sarah Selby (as woman), Tom Jacobs (as waiter)

"Joey, the Patient" (10/4/64)

Synopsis: Joey has to have his tonsils taken out, and his two doctors decide to teach him a lesson for making jokes at their expense.

Written by: Douglas Morrow

Directed by: Mel Ferber

Produced by: Charles Stewart

Cast: Joey Bishop, Abby Dalton, Corbett Monica, Joe Besser, Mary Treen, Richard Keith (as Benny Harwell), Tim Herbert (as Dr. Fisher), Dave Ketchem (as Dr. Marks), Karen Norris (as the nurse), Joey Forman (as Dr. Nolan), Matthew David Smith

"Joey vs. Oscar Levant" (10/11/64)

Synopsis: Joey is dismayed to learn that Oscar Levant, the most disliked tenant in his apartment house, is to be his houseguest.

"Joey and Larry Split" (10/18/64)

Synopsis: Joey and Larry's long friendship almost breaks up when Joey forgets he promised Larry to wish his girlfriend a happy birthday on his TV show.

"In This Corner, Jan Murray" (10/25/64)

Synopsis: Joey and guest star Jan Murray agree to put on a comedy boxing show for charity, but it turns into a real-life grudge match.

Written by: Dick Conway and Roland MacLane

Directed by: Mel Ferber

Produced by: Charles Stewart

Cast: Joey Bishop, Abby Dalton, Corbett Monica, Joe Besser, Mary Treen, Jan Murray, Barbara Stuart (as Toni Murray), Joey Giamba (as the fighter)

"The Nielsen Box" (11/1/64)

Synopsis: Hilda gets a Nielsen box installed on her TV set, which will be used to measure TV ratings. So Joey tries to get on her good side, hoping she will keep her set tuned to his show.

Written by: Sam Loske and Joel Rapp

Directed by: Jerry Paris

Produced by: Charles Stewart

Cast: Joey Bishop, Abby Dalton, Corbett Monica, Mary Treen, Orville Sherman (as Herman), Matthew David Smith

"You're What, Again?" (11/8/64)

Synopsis: Ellie learns that she's pregnant again—but puts off telling Joey because he was so nervous the first time around.

Written by: Garry Marshall and Jerry Belson

Directed by: Mel Ferber

Produced by: Charles Stewart

Cast: Joey Bishop, Abby Dalton, Corbett Monica, Mary Treen, Joey Forman (as Dr. Nolan)

"Joey Goes to a Poker Party" (11/15/64)

Synopsis: Joey comes home late from a poker party and tries to set the clock back so Ellie will think it's earlier than it is. But Joey doesn't know that Ellie is aware of this trick.

Written by: Dale McRaven and Carl Kleinschmitt

Directed by: Mel Ferber

Produced by: Charles Stewart

Cast: Joey Bishop, Abby Dalton, Corbett Monica, Allan Melvin (as Bernie), Herkie Styles (as Freddie), Mel Bishop (as Jack), Johnny Silver (as Charlie), Buddy Lewis (as the milkman)

"The Perfect Girl" (11/22/64)

Synopsis: Larry falls hard for a pretty houseguest staying with Joey and Ellie. But when he feels that she wants to marry him, he stops pursuing the relationship and asks Joey to tell her the romance is over.

Written by: Carl Kleinschmitt and Dale McRaven

Directed by: Mel Ferber

Produced by: Charles Stewart

Cast: Joey Bishop, Abby Dalton, Corbett Monica, Joe Besser, Mary Treen, Shirley Bonne (as Liz)

"Joey's Courtship" (11/29/64)

Synopsis: Joey tries to give Larry the benefit of his expert experience with romance, but the whole thing blows up in his face when he discovers that Ellie is bitter because Joey never really courted her before their marriage.

Written by: Charles Stewart

Directed by: Mel Ferber

Produced by: Charles Stewart

Cast: Joey Bishop, Abby Dalton, Corbett Monica, Joe Besser, Mary Treen, Allan Melvin (as the policeman)

"Ellie Goes to Court" (12/6/64)

Synopsis: Ellie gets a traffic ticket for an illegal left turn but insists that she is innocent. So she goes to court to defend herself.

Written by: Dale McRaven and Carl Kleinschmitt

Directed by: Mel Ferber

Produced by: Charles Stewart

Cast: Joey Bishop, Abby Dalton, Corbett Monica, Joe Besser, Mary Treen, Parley Baer (as the judge), Stacy Harris (as the prosecutor), Robert "Bobby" Johnson (as the bailiff), Mel Bishop (as the court clerk), Bill Bradley (as the policeman)

"Jillson's Toupee" (12/13/64)

Synopsis: Joey gives Jillson a toupee as a gift, causing Jillson to undergo a surprising personality change. Tenants in the building start complaining that Jillson is too busy admiring himself to do any work, but he says he'd rather lose his job than lose his new hair.

Written by: Carl Kleinschmit and Dale McRaven

Directed by: Mel Ferber

Produced by: Charles Stewart

Cast: Joey Bishop, Abby Dalton, Corbett Monica, Joe Besser, Mary Treen, William Keene (as the salesman), Sarah Selby (as Iris), Robert Carson (as Jim), Tom Jacobs (as the customer), Joey Forman (as Dr. Nolan), Matthew David Smith

"A Hobby for Ellie" (12/29/64)

Synopsis: Joey becomes concerned that Ellie will endanger her pregnancy by doing the housework, so he takes over all the chores. Joey and Larry then decide that Ellie needs to pick a hobby, but they disagree on what it should be.

Written by: Iz Elinson and Fred S. Fox

Directed by: Mel Ferber

Produced by: Charles Stewart

Cast: Joey Bishop, Abby Dalton, Corbett Monica

"Rusty Arrives" (1/5/65)

Synopsis: Joey's nephew, Rusty Williams (Rusty Hamer from *Make Room for Daddy*) comes to live with Joey and Ellie. They're expecting Rusty to be the typical wild teenager and are surprised by how well-behaved he is.

Written by: Carl Kleinshmit and Dale McRaven

Directed by: Mel Ferber

Produced by: Charles Stewart

Cast: Joey Bishop, Abby Dalton, Corbett Monica, Mary Treen, Rusty Hamer, Matthew David Smith

"The Weed City Story" (1/12/65)

Synopsis: Guest star Cliff Arquette plays a whistle-stop hotel operator who resorts to every conceivable device to keep Joey in town long enough to officiate at a post office groundbreaking ceremony.

"Rusty's Education" (1/19/65)

Synopsis: Rusty begins college and keeps asking Joey questions that Joey can't answer because he never went to college. Embarrassed at his lack of education, he and Larry ask for help from a convicted bookmaker with a photographic mind.

Written by: Dale McRaven and Carl Kleinshmitt

Directed by: Mel Ferber

Produced by: Charles Stewart

Cast: Joey Bishop, Abby Dalton, Corbett Monica, Joe Besser, Mary Treen, Charles Cantor (as Inagain Finnegan), Peter Leeds (as Bernie Stern), Alan Melvin (as Sgt. McCormick), Rusty Hamer (as Rusty)

"The Sultan's Gift" (1/26/65)

Synopsis: Joey entertains at an official luncheon honoring a visiting sultan, who expresses his appreciation by sending Joey a couple of harem beauties—much to Ellie's dismay.

Written by: Jerry Belson

Directed by: Mel Ferber

Produced by: Charles Stewart

Cast: Joey Bishop, Abby Dalton, Corbett Monica, Mary Treen, Frank Wilcox (as Charles Clayton), Mickey Simpson (as Punjab), Ray Kellogg (as Danjab). Harem girls: Pat Winters, Merissa Matha.

"Joey Entertains Rusty's Fraternity" (2/2/65)

Synopsis: Joey and three pals help Rusty and his fellow pledges carry out an unusual fraternity initiation stunt—by dressing like girls and going to a fraternity dance.

Written by: Dale McRaven and Carl Kleinschmitt

Directed by: Mel Ferber

Produced by: Charles Stewart

Cast: Joey Bishop, Abby Dalton, Corbett Monica, Mary Treen, Rusty Hamer, Cliff Norton, Joey Forman (as Dr. Nolan), Rick Newton (as frat president), Craig Marshall (as pledge), Darryl Richards (as pledge), Mike Winkelman (as pledge)

"The Do-It-Yourself Nursery" (2/9/65)

Synopsis: Joey takes on the chore of converting a spare room into a nursery after his unending barrage of chatter and unsolicited advice forces the workmen he hired to quit the job.

Written by: Dale McRaven and Carl Kleinschmitt

Directed by: Mel Ferber

Produced by: Charles Stewart

Cast: Joey Bishop, Abby Dalton, Corbett Monica, Mary Treen, Herbie Faye (as Krupnik)

"The Sergeant's Testimonial" (2/16/65)

Synopsis: Joey refuses to attend a reunion of his wartime Army outfit when he learns that his sadistic former master sergeant will be the guest of honor.

Written by: Carl Kleinshmitt and Dale McRaven

Directed by: Mel Ferber

Produced by: Charles Stewart

Cast: Joey Bishop, Abby Dalton, Corbett Monica, Joe Besser, Mary Treen, Cliff Norton (as Al), Allan Melvin (as Art)

"Joey Changes Larry's Luck" (2/23/65)

Synopsis: Habitual loser Larry suddenly wins during an evening of carefully rigged poker and decides to parlay his hot streak into a fortune for himself and his friends.

Written by: Dale McRaven and Carl Kleinschmitt

Directed by: Mel Ferber

Produced by: Charles Stewart

Cast: Joey Bishop, Corbett Monica, Mary Treen, Alan Melvin (as Art), Cliff Norton (as Al), Gene Baylos (first waiter), Lenny Kent (second waiter), Myrna Ross (as cashier), Mel Bishop (as customer), Ronnie Martin (as customer)

"Never Put it in Writing" (3/2/65)

Synopsis: Joey's generosity is misinterpreted when he tries to reward Larry for his long years of faithful service by giving him his own office and hiring another writer to help him. Larry, however, thinks that this means that Joey is trying to get rid of him.

Written by: James Allandice and Tom Adair and Dale McRaven and Carl Kleinschmitt

Directed by: Mel Ferber

Produced by: Charles Stewart

Cast: Joey Bishop, Corbett Monica, Joe Besser, Mary Treen, Bob Watson (as Bernie Stern)

"Larry's Habit" (3/9/65)

Synopsis: Larry stays in Joey's apartment to keep him company while Ellie is away and nearly drives him to distraction by cracking his knuckles.

Written by: Carl Kleinschmitt and Dale McRaven

Story by: Sam Locke and Joel Rapp

Directed by: Mel Ferber

Produced by: Charles Stewart

Cast: Joey Bishop, Corbett Monica, Joe Besser, Mary Treen, Alan Melvin (as Art), Frank Wilcox (as Dr. Rangle)

"Joey, the Star Maker" (3/16/65)

Synopsis: Joey generously lauds a friend's wife for her performance in an amateur production—and then finds himself being coerced into putting her on his own television show.

Written by: Garry Marshall and Jerry Belson

Directed by: Mel Ferber

Produced by: Charles Stewart

Cast: Joey Bishop, Joe Besser, Mary Treen, Barbara Stuart (as Dorothy Miller), Alan Melvin (as Art), Robert S. Carson (as Mr. Beatty), Herkie Styles (as clapboard man), JacQueline Russell (as "housewife A"), Tom McDonough (as the cameraman)

"What'll You Have?" (3/23/65)

Synopsis: Joey and Ellie are throwing a party when one of the guests asks Ellie what she thinks the new baby will be. When Ellie says she thinks it will be a girl, Joey argues and says he thinks it will be another boy—and then Ellie suddenly goes into labor and has a little girl.

Written by: Carl Kleinschmitt and Dale McRaven

Directed by: Mel Ferber

Produced by: Charles Stewart

Cast: Joey Bishop, Abby Dalton, Corbett Monica, Joe Besser, Mary Treen, Barbara Stuart (as Dorothy Miller), Alan Melvin (as Art), Louise Glenn (as Alice Nolan), JacQueline Russell (as the nurse), Johnny Silver (as Mr. Beaumont), Joey Forman (as Dr. Nolan), Kathleen Kinmont Smith (as the new baby girl)

Author's Note: Kathleen Kinmont Smith was the real-life daughter of Abby Dalton.

"Joey Discovers Jackie Clark" (3/30/65)

Synopsis: Joey, who "discovers" comedian Jackie Clark, finds out that Jackie's mother doesn't want her son to be in show business.

THE JOEY BISHOP SHOW

Network: ABC

Format: 90 minutes, Monday through Friday

Premiere: April 17, 1967

Finale: November 25, 1969

Host: Joey Bishop

Announcer/sidekick: Regis Philbin

Band: Johnny Mann and His Merry Men

Also featuring: Jack Riley, Mark London, Joe Besser, Joanne Worley, Ann Elder

Onionhead (1958)

Plot synopsis: In this sequel of sorts to *No Time for Sergeants,* which was also released in 1958, Andy Griffith plays hillbilly recruit Al Woods, working as a ship's cook in the U.S. Coast Guard. Joey played Gutsell, his wisecracking shipmate.

Directed by: Norman Taurog

Written by: Nelson Gidding and Weldon Hill

Produced by: Jules Schermer

Cast:
  Andy Griffith: Al Woods
  Felicia Farr: Stella
  Walter Matthau: "Red" Wildoe
  Erin O'Brien: Jo Hill
  Joe Mantell: "Doc" O'Neal
  Ray Danton: Ensign Dennis Higgins
  James Gregory: The Skipper
  Joey Bishop: Gutsell
  Roscoe Karns: "Windy" Woods
  Claude Akins: Poznicki
  Ainslie Pryor: Chief Miller
  Sean Garrison: Yeoman Kaffhamp
  Mark Roberts: Lieutenant Bennett
  Tige Andrews: Charlie Berger

The Deep Six (1958)

Plot synopsis: Alan Ladd, who also produced, plays a Quaker who is forced to overcome his beliefs in non-violence when he's drafted into service during World War II and assigned to submarine duty. Eventually he triumphs and, in the process, becomes a war hero.

Directed by: Rudolph Maté

Written by: Harry Brown, Martin Dibner, Martin Rackin and John Twist

Produced by: Alan Ladd, Martin Rackin

Cast:
    Alan Ladd: Alec Austen
    Dianne Foster: Susan Cahill
    William Bendix: "Frenchy" Shapiro
    Keenan Wynn: Lieutenant Commander Mike Edge
    James Whitmore: Commander Meredith
    Efrem Zimbalist Jr: Lieutenant Blanchard
    Joey Bishop: Ski Krokowski
    Barbara Eiler: Claire Innes
    Ross Bagdasarian: Aaron Slobodjian
    Jeanette Nolan: Mrs. Austen
    Walter Reed: Paul Clemson
    Peter Hansen: Lieutenant Dooley
    Richard Crane: Lieutenant Swanson
    Jerry Mathers: Steve Innes

The Naked and the Dead (1958)

Plot synopsis: Adapted from Norman Mailer's best-selling novel, *The Naked and the Dead* recounts the good, the bad, and the ugly in a battalion fighting in the South Pacific during World War II.

Directed by: Raoul Walsh

Written by: Norman Mailer (based on his novel), Denis Sanders and Terry Sanders

Produced by: Paul Gregory

Cast:
Aldo Ray: Sergeant Croft
Cliff Robertson: Lieutenant Hearn
Raymond Massey: General Cummings
Lili St. Cyr: Lily
Barbara Nichols: Mildred
William Campbell: Brown
Richard Jaeckel: Gallagher
James Best: Rhidges
Joey Bishop: Private Roth
Jerry Paris: Goldstein
Robert Gist: Red
L.Q. Jones: Wilson
John Beradino: Mantelli

Pepe (1960)

Plot synopsis: Cantinflas stars as a Mexican peasant who travels to Hollywood seeking fame and fortune. The movie was notable only for the many stars (see below) who played themselves in cameos. Joey's only line in the movie? "Son of a gun!"

Directed by: George Sidney

Written by: Claude Binyon, Leslie Bush-Fekete, Dorothy Kingsley, Sonya Levien and Leonard Spigelgass

Produced by: George Sidney

Cast:
Cantinflas: Pepe
Dan Dailey: Ted Holt
Shirley Jones: Suzie Murphy
Cameos: Joey Bishop, Maurice Chevalier, Bing Crosby, Richard Conte, Bobby Darin, Sammy Davis Jr., Jimmy Durante, Zsa Zsa Gabor, Judy Garland, Greer Garson, Hedda Hopper, Ernie Kovacs, Peter Lawford, Janet Leigh, Jack Lemmon, Jay North, Kim Novak, André Previn, Donna Reed, Debbie Reynolds, Edward G. Robinson, Cesar Romero, Frank Sinatra, Tony Curtis, Dean Martin, Carlos Montalbán

Ocean's 11 (1960)

Plot synopsis: War veteran Danny Ocean (Frank Sinatra) recruits ten of his Army buddies for the heist-of-a-lifetime: robbing all the major Las Vegas casinos simultaneously during a power blackout. *Ocean's 11* is viewed by most critics (and fans) as the ultimate Rat Pack flick, since it was filmed in Las Vegas in January and February 1960 at the same time as the Rat Pack's "Summit" shows at The Sands Hotel.

Directed by: Lewis Milestone

Written by: George Clayton Johnson, Jack Golden Russell, Harry Brown, and Charles Lederer

Produced by: Lewis Milestone

Cast:
Frank Sinatra: Danny Ocean
Dean Martin: Sam Harmon
Sammy Davis Jr.: Josh Howard
Peter Lawford: Jimmy Foster
Joey Bishop: Mushy O'Connors
Angie Dickinson: Beatrice Ocean
Richard Conte: Anthony Bergdorf
Cesar Romero: Duke Santos
Patrice Wymore: Adele Ekstrom
Akim Tamiroff: Spyros Acebos
Henry Silva: Roger Corneal
Ilka Chase: Mrs. Restes
Buddy Lester: Vince Massler
Richard Benedict: Curly Stephans
Norman Fell: Peter Reimer
Cameos: Red Skelton, George Raft, Rummy Bishop, Nicky Blair, Hoot Gibson, Pinky Lee, Shirley MacLaine, Red Norvo

Johnny Cool (1963)

Plot synopsis: A Sicilian bandit (Henry Silva) is trained by a retired American gangster and sent back to the U.S. to exact vengeance on the gangster's sworn enemies.

Directed by: William Asher

Written by: Joseph Landon, John McPartland (from his novel *The Kingdom of Johnny Cool*)

Produced by: William Asher, Peter Lawford

Cast:
Henry Silva: Johnny Cool/Giordano
Elizabeth Montgomery: Dare Guiness
Richard Anderson: Correspondent
Jim Backus: Louis Murphy

Joey played a used-car salesman in Johnny Cool *opposite Elizabeth Montgomery. He took the role as a favor to executive producer Peter Lawford, who had fallen out of favor with Sinatra.*

Joey Bishop: Used car salesman
Brad Dexter : Lennart Crandall
John McGiver: Oby Hinds
Gregory Morton: Jerry March
Mort Sahl: Ben Morrow
Telly Savalas: Vince Santangelo
Sammy Davis Jr.: "Educated"
Elisha Cook Jr.: Undertaker

Sergeants 3 (1962)

Plot synopsis: A variation on *Gunga Din*, Rat Pack style, *Sergeants 3* marked the last time Peter Lawford would ever work with Frank Sinatra. The movie, shot in Kanab, Utah, during the summer of 1962, revolved around three Civil War cavalry sergeants (Sinatra, Dean Martin, and Lawford) and their ex-slave bugler (Sammy Davis Jr.) who encounter some hostile Indians. "The participants have a better time than the onlookers," sniffed movie critic Judith Crist in her review of *Sergeants 3*.

Directed by: John Sturges

Written by: W. R. Burnett

Produced by: Frank Sinatra

Cast:

Frank Sinatra: Mike Merry
Dean Martin: Sergeant Chip Deal
Sammy Davis Jr.: Jonah Williams
Peter Lawford: Sergeant Larry Barrett
Joey Bishop: Roger Boswell
Henry Silva: Mountain Hawk
Ruta Lee: Amelia Parent
Buddy Lester: Willie Sharpknife

Texas Across the River (1966)

Plot synopsis: Texas cowboy Sam Hollis and his Indian sidekick, Kronk, meet up with a dashing Mexican Count and embark on a series of misadventures.

Directed by: Michael Gordon

Written by: Wells Root, Harold Green and Ben Starr

Produced by: Harry Keller

Cast:
> Dean Martin: Sam Hollis
> Alain Delon: Don Andrea
> Joey Bishop: Kronk
> Rosemary Forsyth: Phoebe
> Peter Graves: Captain Stimpson
> Michael Ansara: Iron Jacket
> Andrew Prine: Lieutenant Sibley

A Guide for the Married Man (1967)

Plot synopsis: A self-styled philanderer (Robert Morse) tries to teach his straight-laced neighbor (Walter Matthau) how to cheat on his wife and *not* get caught.

Directed by: Gene Kelly

Written by: Franklin Tarloff (from his book)

Produced by: Frank McCarthy

Cast:
> Walter Matthau: Paul Manning
> Inger Stevens: Ruth Manning
> Robert Morse: Ed Stander
> Sue Anne Langdon: Mrs. Johnson
> Cameos: Lucille Ball, Jack Benny, Polly Bergen, Joey Bishop,

Ben Blue, Sid Caesar, Art Carney, Wally Cox, Jeffrey Hunter, Jayne Mansfield, Carl Reiner, Phil Silvers, Terry-Thomas

Valley of the Dolls (1967)

Plot synopsis: Adapted from Jacqueline Susann's controversial novel, *Valley of the Dolls* tells the story of three innocent young actresses who are corrupted by the sleazy underbelly of show-biz and eventually fall prey to drugs and overindulgence.

Directed by: Mark Robson

Written by: Helen Deutsch, Dorothy Kinglsey (from the novel by Jacqueline Susann)

Produced by: David Weisbart

Cast:
    Barbara Parkins: Anne Welles
    Patty Duke: Neely O'Hara
    Paul Burke: Lyon Burke
    Sharon Tate: Jennifer North
    Martin Milner: Mel Anderson
    Joey Bishop: Emcee at telethon
    George Jessel: Emcee at Grammy Awards

Who's Minding the Mint? (1967)

Plot synopsis: A U.S. Mint worker (Jim Hutton) accidentally loses $50,000 and recruits a group of ragtag misfits to help him break into the mint at night and replace the lost money.

Directed by: Howard Morris

Written by: R. S. Allen, Harvey Bullock

Produced by: Norman Maurer

Cast:
    Jim Hutton: Harry Lucas
    Dorothy Provine: Verna Baxter
    Milton Berle: Luther Burton
    Joey Bishop: Ralph Randazzo
    Bob Denver: Willie Owens
    Walter Brennan: Pop Gillis
    Victor Buono: Captain
    Jack Gilford: Avery Dugan
    Jamie Farr: Mario

The Delta Force (1986)

Plot synopsis: An American jetliner is hijacked by Palestinian terrorists and diverted to Beirut. The Pentagon sends in its elite group of Delta

Force commandos, led by Major Scott McCoy (Chuck Norris), to save the day.

Directed by: Menahem Golan

Written by: James Bruner, Menahem Golan

Produced by: Menhem Golan

Cast:

    Chuck Norris: Major Scott McCoy
    Lee Marvin: Colonel Nick Alexander
    Martin Balsam: Ben Kaplan
    Joey Bishop: Harry Goldman
    Robert Forster: Abdul
    Lainie Kazan: Sylvia Goldman
    George Kennedy: Father O'Malley
    Robert Vaughn: General Woodbridge
    Shelley Winters: Edie Kaplan
    Bo Svenson: Captain Campbell

Betsy's Wedding (1990)

Plot synopsis: An eccentric family, led by patriarch Eddie Hopper (Alan Alda), prepares for their daughter's wedding amidst a backdrop of comedic chaos and confusion.

Directed by: Alan Alda

Written by: Alan Alda

Produced by: Martin Bregman

Cast:

    Alan Alda: Eddie Hopper
    Joey Bishop: Eddie's father
    Madeline Kahn: Lola Hopper
    Anthony LaPaglia: Stevie Dee
    Catherine O'Hara: Gloria Henner
    Joe Pesci: Oscar Henner
    Molly Ringwald: Betsy Hopper
    Ally Sheedy: Connie Hopper
    Burt Young: Georgie

Mad Dog Time (1996)

Plot synopsis: A Mob boss is back in business after a stint in the loony bin and has to deal with enemies gunning for his territory.

Directed by: Larry Bishop

Written by: Larry Bishop

Cast:
  Henry Silva: Sleepy Joe Carlisle
  Michael J. Pollard: Red Mash
  Joey Bishop: Mr. Gottlieb
  Richard Dreyfuss: Vic
  Burt Reynolds: "Wacky" Jacky Jackson
  Richard Pryor: Jimmie the Grave
  Also: Ellen Barkin, Gabriel Byrne, Jeff Goldblum, Gregory Hines, Billy Idol, Rob Reiner